Release

Your

Healing

Release

Your

Healing

You deliverance is in the detail

Dr.Andrew David

Release Your Healing © 2019 by Dr. Andrew David

ISBN: 9781701271647

Independently published

Author email: releaseyourhealing@gmail.com

Dedications

I dedicate this book to my wife Nisha and our children Samuel and Ruth.

Nisha, you are God's gift to me. Without your love and patience, I don't know if I could have walked my healing journey. I am ever grateful for all your sacrifices and expression of unconditional love. I am a blessed man!

Samuel and Ruth, you are both precious to dad. You teach me so many things which amaze me. Your faith has been an inspiration to me. No wonder Jesus talked about *child like faith!* Keep believing and keep speaking faith, because daddy is learning from you.

All things are possible to him who believes!

–Jesus

Table of Contents

Introduction

The message in this book revolves around the truth about the death, burial, and the resurrection of Jesus Christ. The healing of your body and mind which you fervently seek is woven in the revelation of the cross of Jesus Christ. In this book I have systematically unpacked the truth about your true identity.

I suffered for several years in my life because I did not understand the finished work of Jesus on the cross. My prayers were not grounded in the New Covenant realities. I simply did not know who *I am* in Him. I have not yet come to fully grasp this, but I left the place of ignorance where I used to be. You too will start this incredible journey of finding your true identity: Your completeness in Him! My life was a defeated life for a very long time. What I mean by that is, I was addicted to sinful habits, and was also sick in my body. There was a monumental gap between what the Bible claimed to offer and what I was experiencing in my life. I knew He had the answer but I just didn't know how to get it from Him. It was at a time of utter despair I turned to the Lord more earnestly. I kept seeking Him and then one day the scales fell off my eyes. I was meditating on the book of Romans chapter 6 to chapter 8, and I saw the cross of Christ for the first time in my heart. The work of God on the cross is a marvellous work of Grace. The revelation of the cross is the most important revelation that is needed for every believer. Now, I want to tell the whole world what Jesus did on the cross for them, especially to those who are struggling with sickness in their bodies and minds.

This book is broadly divided into two sections. In section A, I have elaborated about the condition of the heart after the fall of man and how Jesus had fixed it. The death, burial, and the resurrection of Jesus are the most important revelation every believer needs for victorious living in every area of their life. Sadly, many don't know what happened on the cross. Only a vague sense of Jesus taking their sins away is what most of the believers understand about the cross. Though that is true in every sense, there is more depth to it! This revelation is the key that unlocks everything you can receive from God. Remember, God has done His part. Now we have to engage in the process of renewing our mind to actuate what has been freely given to us. This book will teach you how to do just that. The first five chapters go into detail about what happened on the cross, and because of that what has happened to us when we first believed. Because of the cross, you can live a life of victory, and overcome sickness, demons or any other adversity that you are currently facing. Section A focuses on accurate information about the death, burial and the resurrection of Jesus Christ. Again, giving you accurate information alone is not my primary aim. Hence, Section B.

In Section B, the information you have gained will be transformed into reality when you engage in the process detailed inside. In this section, you will understand more about how to connect with the cross and experience resurrection power. You will learn more about communing with God in your heart. God is a *heart* God! God lives in our hearts. The heart of the man is the new Holy of Holies. The tabernacle of the Old Testament was a picture of the man. The true temple of the Holy Spirit is the man himself. The spirit of the man is the new Holy of Holies. God abides in our spirit! Unless we learn to commune with Him in our hearts, we don't know how to experience eternal life. Ignorantly, we are trying to move God assuming that He is somewhere up there in the heavens. But the truth is He lives in the new Holy of Holies, which is our heart. What we need to do is to learn how to enter into the secret place of the most high and commune with Him. The veil that is stopping us from seeing God is our carnal mind. Remember, only we can tear the veil of our carnal mind. When we tear that veil, then we can see God as He is in our spirit. The resurrection power of Jesus is locked-up inside us in our spirit! We need to learn how to release it otherwise we will miss out on experiencing God's life. The 'mighty move' believers everywhere are eagerly waiting for is actually inside every spirit-filled Christian. Your healing is inside you as you are about to find out and actuate it.

Endnotes

Every chapter has scripture reference numbered at the end. The number corresponds to the number that is in *superscript* in the text of the chapter.

Read This First

You picked up this book because you have not given up hope on God's word, and you want to experience healing in your physical body and your mind. Probably your health has been worrying you. You have prayed and confessed all the healing scriptures relentlessly like the others who have testified before you. Maybe, it has not worked for you. What am I doing wrong? This question burns within your soul. If you are sick and tired of being sick and tired, you are ready to leap into this incredible journey. I firmly believe that God has placed this book in your hands because He loves you and wants you to experience the truth. This book will not show you what's wrong about you; rather, it will show you what has been made right about you. In this book you will find yourself taking on a journey. A journey you have been destined to travel like the renowned men and women of the Bible. Many have travelled this road before and still others like me are discovering this road on a daily basis, a road that is least travelled. Jesus said that many are those who take the road that leads to destruction, but only a few will find the road that leads to life[1]. You are going to find that road!

You will receive your healing during this study, but I intend to take you beyond that. I want you to see how God desires that you walk in divine health by experiencing who you are in Him. You will be transformed by the truth as you understand and apply the truth in your life. This transformation will be a painless transformation.

> I went by the field of the lazy man, And by the vineyard of the man devoid of understanding; And there it was all overgrown with thorns, Its surface was covered with nettles; Its stone wall was broken down.
>
> Proverbs 24: 30-31 NKJV

Sickness and disease are like thorns and nettles in our lives. The vineyard of our life is destroyed and its stone walls are broken. Wisdom says that this destruction is because of a lack of understanding and a lazy man will not take time to gain understanding. It has been said, ignorance is bliss! No, it's not bliss; rather, ignorance is killing us and taking us into captivity[2]. The one thing that God said that will keep His children in captivity is the lack of knowledge[3]. The word *captivity* means to get trapped or to get arrested. We are trapped in sickness and disease and this is oftentimes because of our lack of knowledge more than anything else. In the Hebrew language ignorance is compared to darkness. The power of Satan is our ignorance of the truth. In the parable of the sower, Jesus said he who accepted the word and understands it, it is he who will bring forth a great harvest[4].

David was one of the greatest kings of Israel who loved the Lord all his days. His son Solomon was the wisest and richest king who ever reigned in Israel after David. Solomon received many instructions from his father growing up under his care. One such instruction is this,

Wisdom is the principal thing; Therefore get wisdom.

And in all your getting, get understanding.

Proverbs 4:7 NKJV

The issue of understanding is related to the heart. The Bible says that God sent His word and healed and delivered His people from all destruction[5]. God loves His children and desires that they walk in divine health and prosperity[6], and to this cause He gave the Word. His word when received with faith in the heart and applied in our life, will produce what it says. God's word will produce healing in your body! The wisdom Jesus gave to the church is to study and understand His word. This understanding is not a mere mental grasp of the information. It's an intentional study of the truth to the point that it becomes part of one's identity. Man was not designed to live by food alone, but by every word that proceeds from the mouth of God. A born again believer who is deviating from the Word of God will soon wither away because he is deviating from his or her life source.

Like how the Apostle Paul exhorted Timothy to meditate on God's word and to give himself entirely to the word[7], we too should commit ourselves entirely to studying God's word. You will never regret it! A disciple is someone who wants to live as the master lives. It requires commitment! So in this book, I encourage you to commit to learn and understand His ways. With that commitment, you are ready to move on.

Jesus said to His disciples to be careful about what they were hearing. The measure of thought and study they gave to the truth they heard will be the measure of virtue and knowledge that comes back to them and much more will be given to them (Mark 4:24 AMP *Paraphrased*). God is not saying; "If you spend more time with me I will bless you more." No! Rather, if we spend more time with Him, we increase our capacity to experience Him more! The ball is in our court, metaphorically speaking.

> My son, pay attention to what I say; turn your ear to my words. Do not let them out of your sight; keep them within your heart; for they are life to those who find them and **health** to one's whole body. Proverbs 4:23, NIV, emphasis mine

Health is found in God's word and moreover His word can drive sickness out of your body. The word *health* in the above verse is translated from the Hebrew word which means *medicine*. Today's modern medicine has many negative side-effects. Sometimes the side-effects are worse than the disease itself. However, unlike modern medicines, God's word has no negative side-effects, rather positive ones!

I have approached some truths from various angles in this book. Some truths like our identity in Christ, biblical meditation, walking in the spirit are worth studying in detail; because they are the keys to actuate your healing, and maintain health. No matter how bad your situation is, it can be changed! All one needs to do is learn to how to believe.

Jesus said that all things are possible to him who believes. If somethings are not possible for me, it only means that I have not learnt how to believe for it.

Like it or not, we are a product of our society. The society that we live in has a strong influence in our subconscious mind. Therefore, when we go counterculture in any area, it needs a greater amount of dedication and focus from our part to bring change in our lives. Change is often threatening to us. The word *repentance* means to change one's mind. Every time when my opinion and God's opinion are at opposition, I need to lay down my opinion and take his opinion as mine. This is what repentance is and this is the way of a disciple.

In the story of the woman with the issue of blood who touched the hem of the garment of Jesus to receive her healing, the Bible records this: "for she had been saying to herself, "If I only touch His outer robe, I will be healed." (Matthew 9:21, AMP). This is what meditation is all about. She kept rolling that thought over and over in her head. "Saying to her-self" means self-talk. She was talking about the end result more than her problem that was threatening her. The voice that has the most powerful influence in your life is your own voice. This has been the way of life for the psalmist David, because many psalms are nothing more than self-talks. I believe this should be the way of life for us too if we want to change our lives for the good. Society and social media are full of negative voices. If we are not careful to filter them out, we will succumb to their negative influence over our lives.

The ONLY aspect of Christian living the Bible promotes consistently is the aspect of WALKING IN THE SPIRIT. From Genesis to Revelation that is the one core message of the Bible. The Apostle Paul said the spirit lusts against the flesh and the flesh lusts against the spirit[8]. The greatest challenge you will face in your life is the challenge to change your fixed non-biblical pattern of thinking. To be carnally minded is death, but to be spiritually-minded is life and peace. Deliverance in the area of sickness is easy when you learn how to walk in the spirit. The entire construction of this book is to encourage you to see this truth. In this book you will also learn more about the heart because your heart is your true identity. You will also learn how healing has to first and foremost start in your heart. Walking in the spirit is intricately linked to the condition of your heart. This book will also show you how to influence your heart positively and permanently with God's word. It is important to understand the brokenness of the heart of the fallen man and how Jesus offers to fix it. One can never fix their issues of life by their own strength, and that was the reason Christ offered His life for us to make it our own; you will understand this further along. People with broken hearts do not have a healthy sense of boundary and therefore they cannot perceive where they stop and others begin. A broken heart is the root cause of all sickness and diseases! As born again Christians, our hearts can also be broken over the issues of life. However, when that happens, we should know how to redeem ourselves. The cross is not a onetime experience in the life of a believer. It is an everyday experience for redemption, one situation at a time. This is why the Bible says Christ has become unto us redemption (1 Corinthians 1:30). Only in Him are we complete, and this is the beginning and the end of the whole matter.

Reference and Endnotes

1. "Enter by the narrow gate; for wide *is* the gate and broad *is* the way that leads to destruction, and there are many who go in by it. Because narrow *is* the gate and difficult *is* the way which leads to life, and there are few who find it. Matthew 7: 13-14 NKJV.
   This scripture is often taught as, "many are going to hell and only few are going to heaven." But if you see the context in which Jesus is teaching, He is talking about principles of Kingdom living. You will understand this during the course of the study.

2. My people are destroyed for lack of knowledge. Because you have rejected knowledge... Hosea 4:6a NKJV.

3. Therefore my people have gone into captivity, Because *they have* no knowledge; Their honourable men *are* famished, And their multitude dried up with thirst. Isaiah 5:13 NKJV

4. "Therefore hear the parable of the sower: When anyone hears the word of the kingdom, and does not understand *it,* then the wicked *one* comes and snatches away what was sown in his heart. This is he who received seed by the wayside. But he who received the seed on stony places, this is he who hears the word and immediately receives it with joy; yet he has no root in himself, but endures only for a while. For when tribulation or persecution arises because of the word, immediately he stumbles. [22] Now he who received seed among the thorns is he who hears the word, and the cares of this world and the deceitfulness of riches choke the word, and he becomes unfruitful. But he who received seed on the good ground is he who hears the word and understands *it,* who indeed bears fruit and produces: some a hundredfold, some sixty, some thirty." Matthew 13: 18-23 NKJV *emphasis mine.*

5. He sent His word and healed them, And delivered *them* from their destruction. Psalm 107:20 NKJV.

6. Let them shout for joy and be glad, Who favor my righteous cause; And let them say continually, "Let the LORD be

magnified, Who has pleasure in the prosperity of His servant." Psalm 107: 20 NKJV *emphasis mine.*

7. Meditate on these things; give yourself entirely to them, that your progress may be evident to all. Take heed to yourself and to the doctrine. Continue in them, for in doing this you will save both yourself and those who hear you. 1 Timothy 4:16 NKJV

8. For the flesh lusteth against the Spirit, and the Spirit against the flesh: and these are contrary the one to the other: so that ye cannot do the things that ye would. Galatians 5:17 KJV

A Healing Testimony

I t all changed when my health tumbled down! A dream to establish a successful career, earn money and enjoy life was at threat when I was diagnosed with a chronic health condition. Depression, despair and frustration were raging within me. The God of the Bible reveals Himself as *Jehovah Rapha* (which means the Lord heals) to the Israelites (Exodus 15:22–27). Throughout the Bible, we see the historical record of God's healing power manifest in different periods. Even to this day, there are many healing testimonies around the world witnessing to God's healing power. Waves of revival were birthed out of such supernatural encounters and experiences. Jesus carried our infirmities on His own body on the cross and by His stripes, we are healed! There are many believers in the church, however, who have not received healing in their bodies. They have prayed and believed but it has not worked for them. Why? It never bothered me until I was sick in my own body. The Bible says, hope deferred makes the heart sick (Proverbs 13:12). For many, hope has been deferred in the area of healing and this has caused many to be disappointed with God.

As a medical doctor, I was not paying much attention to divine healing. After all, modern medicine is very sophisticated and has the answer to many diseases. This was my attitude towards sickness and diseases. This mind-set, however, was quickly shaken when I fell sick in my own body with a chronic autoimmune health condition. This led me to years of searching for answers both in the medical books and in the Word of God. I have cried and begged God to heal me, screamed at God in frustration, been through depression, and even desired to end my life a few times. I was in this emotional roller coaster for a long time. So, I come to you with empathy, not only as a doctor but also as a patient myself. My personal experience birthed this book.

I became a born again Christian at the age of 17. Though I was born into a family of churchgoers every Sunday, I could not call myself a disciple of the Lord Jesus until I gave my life to Jesus at the age of 17. Even then, I was only following the Lord Jesus at a distance. I finished my medical degree and a postgraduate diploma in India and moved over to England to pursue a career in the field of Anaesthesiology and Intensive care medicine. I completed my fellowship program, FRCA, in London. It was seven year training in the field of Anaesthesia and Intensive care medicine after which I was qualified to become a consultant. I joined the National Health Services, England, as a consultant in Anaesthesia and Intensive care medicine.

In less than two years of being in the UK, I developed signs and symptoms of inflammatory bowel disease called crohn's disease. It was a very sad day for me and I wept bitterly on the day when I received that diagnosis. All my medical knowledge about the disease plunged me into a state of despair and depression because I knew in my mind it's a chronic condition with no medical cure. At its best, the symptoms can be kept under control with medications. I was quickly put on strong medications like steroids and immunosuppressive medicines. These medications had profound effects on my body.

I was slowly getting used to a new kind of life; on and off strong medications, frequent blood tests, endoscopy tests etc. I started getting side effects to the medication at which point the dosage was regularly altered to find a happy medium. I hated this life and even thought of ending my life a few times. I was married and had children who were a great source of joy in the midst of pain and hopelessness. As life went on I focussed on building my career. I finished my training successfully and became a consultant in the National Health Services, England.

During one of my regular follow up visits to my doctor, one of the consultants said to me that I needed to get used to this kind of life. Deep inside me, there arose a resounding *no*. I heard it clearly in my spirit. Nevertheless, I was getting used to a life of remissions, flare-ups, strong medications, and blood tests amidst a busy career.

WHERE IS GOD WHEN YOU NEED HIM THE MOST?

I have been a Christian since the age of 17. In my view, I had lived a good Christian life since that time. I attended church regularly and was active in many mission works connected to the church. I gave my time and money regularly for God's work. Why has this happened to me? I put on a victim mindset and found myself arguing with God in prayer many times. Maybe God was punishing me for my past sins, maybe I am a bad person, and maybe someone in my family tree was cursed. I was constantly battling with these kinds of thoughts. And where is God when you needed him the most? I turned to numerous Christian friends and Pastors who would pray for me but I was not experiencing healing in my body. Subtly I became cold towards God.

A good friend of mine, who is also a medical doctor, gifted me a DVD of healing testimonies of people who were healed by the power of God. I disregarded that DVD and was not keen on watching it for a long time. One day I had a strong urge in my heart to watch that DVD. As I watched, I saw people testifying to the power of God which they experienced from His word. Many testified that they stood on God's word and received healing in their bodies. From watching those testimonies, I learned something about faith which I had not known before. I realised faith is real and how I was not in faith. Though I was sincere in seeking God, I was sincerely ignorant of God's ways. With renewed hope, I turned to the Lord one **IT IS FROM THE HEART, GOD'S POWER WILL MINISTER TO YOUR BODY.** more time. I humbled myself and prayed sincerely that I am ready to learn from Him. I started my healing journey on that day. Honestly, I cannot tell you when exactly I got well. It came in increments as I kept my focus on Him. I had to fight against years of bad theology, medical knowledge and outright unbelief. God took me on a journey; a life-journey of surrender whereby I not only received healing in my body; but I am also learning to experience the resurrection power of Christ in the other areas of life too. I may not have arrived yet, but I left the place where I used to be. I know deep inside, I am travelling on the right path.

This book is birthed out of this journey. I have written this book with great hope and faith that it will transform your life for good. Actually, when it comes to the Christian way of living, there are only two options, a life of transformation by the power of God or dead religious works. There is no third option! As you read and understand this book, I am confident you will receive healing in your body. But the purpose of this book is not just that, it's about learning to experience the goodness of God in every area of your life starting with health.

God's word is infallible, absolute, perfect, and unshakable. The wisdom Jesus taught us is to apply God's word in our heart. Sadly, that is the one place we have ignored. You will discover the missing link between the power of God and your bodily healing is the *heart*. You will understand God's word is designed to work in your heart! It is from the heart, God's power will minister to your body. Faith works from your heart, a heart that is fully persuaded in the promises of God.

After working for several years as a consultant, God called me to the work of the ministry. So, I resigned from my job as a consultant and now travel around the world; teaching and preaching the good news of Jesus Christ. I also serve my local church as an Associate Pastor. When I share my testimony and minister in the area of healing, I see people connect with the truth and step into the abundant life which Jesus promised.

My friend, I believe my testimony would have rekindled hope in your heart. Now, I want you to commit. A commitment to know the truth! Remember the words of Jesus, "You shall know the truth and the truth will set you free" (John 8:32). This knowledge is not mere mental information, but experiential knowledge. Our goal is to see the truth alive in our hearts and manifest in our lives. This is a call for transformation!

Prayer

Dear Father in Heaven, thank you for guiding me all the days of my life. I may not fully understand at this point why I have been sick but I commit my life and my time once again to you. As I go through this material, please speak to me, and open the eyes of my understanding. Reveal your word to me. I pray that I will come to know the hope of your calling, the riches of your inheritance in me and learn to connect and fellowship with resurrection power.

In Jesus name, I pray. Amen!

If you have sincerely prayed this prayer, wait and watch what God is about to do in your life. Let your healing journey begin!

SECTION A

Chapter 1

GOD'S WILL FOR HEALING

After Jesus finished preaching to a large group of people, He came down from the mountain and a great multitude followed Him. Amidst them, a leper came and worshipped Him saying: "Lord, if you are willing, you can make me clean!" Then Jesus put out His hand and touched him saying: "I am willing, be cleansed!"[1]

The leper understood that Jesus had the power to heal him. He had probably seen from a distance how Jesus healed everyone who went to Him. So, the question in his mind was not whether Jesus had the power to heal or not, but will He use that power to heal his leprosy. It was in those days lepers were untouchables and social outcasts. So, his concern was quite legitimate. With that question in his mind, he approached Jesus. Jesus healed him by touching him and showing him His love and acceptance.

Many people have a similar question: Is it always God's will to heal my physical infirmity? Unless this question is settled in one's heart, one can never move with confident expectation towards God. Hope is a confident expectation of good things, and faith never works without hope. Questions like the above can linger in our head and sometimes cloud our confidence with God. These questions are born out of many genuine negative experiences. We all know at least someone who believed in God for healing and died or is still suffering from sickness. These negative experiences have created a hardness of heart in many believers and some have become quite cynical regarding healing. People pray and throw the ball in God's court and wait for Him to move in His time, anything more than that there is hesitancy. Smith Wigglesworth a mid-19th-century preacher who moved in the mighty power of God said, "Faith leaps but fear hesitates." Hesitation is a dangerous enemy of faith. When I minister to people on the area of healing, the first and foremost question I ask them is, "Are you absolutely sure that it is God's will to heal you?" If they are unsure, then I will

FAITH LEAPS BUT FEAR HESITATES.

show them from the scriptures and bring them to a place where they can see it in the Word of God that it is God's will to heal them. Only after that point, I move forward. Any attempt on my part before clearing that doubt is just a useless exercise that leads nowhere.

GOD REVEALED

In the book of Hebrews, the Bible says that God at various times and in a various manner spoke in times past unto the fathers by the prophets, but in these last days spoken unto us by His Son[2]. The period *these last days* mentioned above started from the time Jesus began to open His mouth to preach about the Kingdom of God. Jesus was the perfect representation of the Father in a human body. In the Old Testament period, the revelation about the nature of God came to men through the prophets. But in Jesus, we have God in the flesh[3]. Jesus is the embodiment of all that God is. The Apostle Paul said that in Him dwells the fullness of the Godhead bodily (Colossians 2:9*).*

WITHOUT JESUS WE DON'T HAVE AN ABSOLUTE REFERENCE POINT FOR KNOWING AND UNDERSTANDING GOD.

Without Jesus, we don't have an absolute reference point for knowing and understanding God. In Jesus, we have a clear picture of who God is and what is His true nature. Any conclusion about God's true nature outside of Jesus is a faulty understanding based on either wrong translation of language or incomplete understanding in our part. The Apostle John makes this point quite clear in the following verse.

No one has seen God [His essence, His divine nature] at any time; the [One and] only begotten God [that is, the unique Son] who is in the intimate presence of the

Father, He has explained Him [and interpreted and revealed the awesome wonder of the Father]. John 1:18 AMP

On the mountain where Jesus was transfigured, His face and His clothes became bright like a noon day Sun; a voice came from heaven crying: "This is my beloved Son, in whom I am well pleased; hear Him[4]." There were Moses and Elijah standing in that mountain along with few of the disciples, but God squarely put His focus on Jesus. Concerning the true nature of God, it is the Son we need to hear! If Jesus is not the place where you look to understand the true nature of God, then you are looking at the wrong place and probably your image of God in your mind is an idol. That image (or idol) might have been constructed using Old Testament scriptures, life experiences or traditional beliefs, nevertheless it's an error! This is an absolute truth! In writing to the church in which some were deviating to agnostic teachings, the Apostle John warns the believers to abstain from building idols in their minds. His firm affirmation, Jesus has come and given an understanding about God and no new revelation is needed![5]

GOD REVEALED HIMSELF THROUGH HIS WORD.

God revealed Himself through His Word in the Old Testament. However, It's only through the life and teachings of Jesus, we can see how that word looked like in real-life practice. All the actions of Jesus were motivated by love because God is love. The Apostle John wrote that God was

The Word from the beginning and Jesus was the Word in the flesh.[6,7]

I write all this to raise this question. Did Jesus heal everyone who came to Him in faith? If your answer is *yes*, then that is God's will for your situation too.

Consider the following scriptures carefully and ponder over it.

> And Jesus went about all Galilee, teaching in their synagogues, and preaching the gospel of the kingdom, and **healing all manner of sickness and all manner of disease among the people.** And his fame went throughout all Syria: and they brought unto him all sick people that were taken with diverse diseases and torments, and those which were possessed with devils, and those which were lunatick, and those that had the palsy; and he healed them. Matthew 4:23, 24 emphasis mine.

> When the even was come, they brought unto him many that were possessed with devils: and he cast out the spirits with his word, and **healed all** that were sick Matthew 8:16 emphasis mine.

> And Jesus went about all the cities and villages, teaching in their synagogues, and preaching the gospel of the kingdom, and **healing every sickness and every disease** among the people. Matthew 9:35, emphasis mine.

> But when Jesus knew it, he withdrew himself from thence: and great multitudes followed him, and **he healed them all**. Matthew 12:15, emphasis mine.

And great multitudes came unto him, having with them those that were lame, blind, dumb, maimed, and many others, and cast them down at Jesus' feet; and **he healed them**. Matthew 15:30, emphasis mine.

And when they were come out of the ship, straightway they knew him. And ran through that whole region roundabout, and began to carry about on beds those that were sick, where they heard he was. And whithersoever he entered, into villages, or cities, or country, they laid the sick in the streets, and besought him that they might touch if it were but the border of his garment: **and as many as touched him were made whole**. Mark 6:54- 56, emphasis mine.

How God anointed Jesus of Nazareth with the Holy Ghost and with power: who went about doing good, and healing ALL that were oppressed of the devil; for God was with him. Acts 10:38, emphasis mine

It is *always God's will to heal you*. We will address how to get healed later. For now, I want you to see this clearly so that there is not an iota of doubt in your mind concerning God's perfect will for your healing. Please take the time to review the above scriptures and contemplate on them. It's time to settle this in your heart once and for all. Don't be in a hurry to read further on. Let God's perfect will become anchored and deeply rooted in your heart. If this is not the starting point, you will never start the journey of persuading your heart. And definitely, you will never arrive.

Now, I want to raise another question: Even though Jesus was God in the flesh, could Jesus heal everyone?... He could not!

Consider the following scriptures.

> So they were offended at Him. But Jesus said to them, "A prophet is not without honour except in his own country and in his own house." **Nor He did not do many mighty works there because of their unbelief**. Matthew 13:57 NKJV, emphasis mine

> And **he could do no mighty work**, save that he laid his hand upon a few sick folk, and healed them. And he marvelled because of their unbelief. And he went around the villages teaching. Mark 6:5-6 NKJV, emphasis mine

The variable was not Jesus. The power of God was available for everyone to access. Therefore the variable was the hearts of men. Many could not see Him beyond His natural body. They were familiar with His family and childhood days[8]. Remember, Jesus looked very ordinary on the outside. The power of God was only in His

IT IS ALWAYS GOD'S WILL TO HEAL YOU.

spirit. Familiarity breeds contempt! As you study this book, you will learn more about the practical definitions of faith and unbelief later. The purpose of this study is to get you to the place of unwavering trust in the promises of God. This is called faith. But I call this *the biblical faith*, which is being fully persuaded in your heart. The Apostle Paul came to this place of being fully persuaded in his heart that He is able to keep what he has committed to Him until that Day of Jesus

Christ[9.] Without coming to that place of full persuasion of the heart, your faith will not work.

My aim in writing this book is to usher you into that place where you are fully persuaded about the goodness of God. When you see who God really is, and how His ways are wonderful and good, and how His burden is light and easy, your heart will be fully persuaded. If we are not studying the Bible for that reason, we are wasting our time. Many times, in our prayer life we are trying to persuade God to agree to our fantasies. The truth is God has already moved by His unfailing love. Christ has died for the sins of the whole world. He has risen. The veil is torn. The invitation is open. The promises are sure. The New Covenant is the only Covenant that is valid before God. They are wrought in Christ! Will you step in? Will you change your mind? You see, *repentance* is when we change our mind. Repentance happens when we surrender our opinions and take up His opinions as our reality. God is waiting for His people to come to this knowledge and yield to His leading. As a loving father, He will always lead us to the green pastures and still waters!

JESUS BECAME A CURSE

The prophet Isaiah saw the sufferings of Jesus on the cross hundreds of years even before the birth of Jesus. Isaiah said how He will be wounded for the sins of the whole world, and by His chastisement He will purchase peace for the whole world[10]. This is the covenant of peace which was prophesied in the Old Testament[11]. The new covenant is God extending peace towards man through Jesus. To purchase that peace Jesus had to become a curse on our behalf on the cross.

Even with all the advancement in medical science, doctors are still perplexed about the origin of many diseases; I would even go to say almost all diseases. Where does sickness come from? In Deuteronomy chapter–28, the blessings and curses attached to the Law of Moses are documented. When you study the curses listed in that chapter, you can see that all forms of sickness are a curse. When I compared this list to a list in the medical textbook, I noticed that all the categories of sickness which is recorded in the medical textbooks are also found in Deuteronomy chapter–28. This curse was brought upon mankind by Adam's sin. Adam's sin gave birth to the flesh! It is through the flesh; Satan finds access to our lives.

Until the Laws and the Commandments came into the world, the whole human race was under the curse. The Law brought sin to light and also brought in a provision for man to temporarily escape from the curses. The Law showed that man was a sinner but the Law could not make any man perfect before God. The only way he can protect himself from the penalty of sin was to offer an animal blood sacrifice. This is why God established animal blood sacrifices in the old covenant laws. These blood sacrifices were types and shadows of Jesus Christ in the old covenant. God in His great love and mercy brought an animal sacrificial system that will temporarily protect man from the tyranny of Satan. If the Law of Moses had not been

THE NEW COVENANT IS THE ONLY COVENANT THAT IS VALID TODAY.

given, there would not have been a Virgin Mary to bring in the Messiah because Satan would have corrupted the bloodline of Jesus[12]. So the Law of Moses put a harness on the effects of sin temporarily. Bringing in the Messiah was the ultimate plan of God for the nation of Israel in the old covenant. God always wanted to save the whole world from the tyranny of sin. John wrote that God loved the whole world that He gave His only begotten son so that whosoever would believe in Him should not perish but have everlasting life (John 3:16). The only way to accomplish this was to bring in a Messiah who will be sacrificed for the entire human race to redeem mankind from sin.

BRINGING IN THE MESSIAH WAS THE ULTIMATE PLAN OF GOD FOR ISRAEL IN THE OLD COVENANT.

The Greek word for salvation is a compound word which also means: to heal, to deliver, to be made whole, to be protected, and to prosper! This is the reason that the work of Jesus Christ on the cross applies both to salvation and healing. This healing is not only an internal heart healing; it also includes our physical bodily healing. The Apostle Paul said that Jesus became a curse by hanging on the tree and delivered us from the curse of the law[13]. The good news of the gospel is that we need not suffer from the effects of the curse. Jesus is our perfect representative on the cross! Now, because we are in Him, we can boldly claim our healing.

HEALING IS YOUR BIRTH-RIGHT

When you are born again, you are born into a new family and with it, come new birth-right. Once addressing a woman who needed healing and deliverance in the gospels, Jesus called healing as, children's bread[14]. Are you a child of God? Then healing is your bread. No loving father will deny bread to their children. How much more does our loving Heavenly Father want His children to walk in divine health? Think about that!

A LIFE OF SURRENDER

A disciple is someone who is just not attempting to know what the teacher knows; he is attempting to live as the master lives. This should be your goal in life too, to live the life Jesus offers. One time a scribe came to Jesus and said to Him, "Teacher, I will follow you wherever you go." And Jesus said to him, "Foxes have holes and birds of the air have nests, but the son of man has nowhere to lay His head"[15]. A student wants to gain intellectual knowledge. But Jesus is not just offering intellectual information. Knowledge puffs up! Jesus is offering way more than what we can desire or ask. He is offering the keys to experience God's life, eternal life in this world here and now. Then another of His disciples said to Him, "Lord let me first go and bury my father," But Jesus said to him, "Follow Me and let the dead bury their own dead." On the surface, a life of surrender

TRUE FREEDOM IS FOUND ONLY IN A SURRENDERED LIFE!

looks scary; feels like pain and misery. But the truth is we are surrendering our flesh life for the spirit-life, we surrender what we held all this time an illusion called "life" for that which is eternal life which God had made available for us in Christ. True freedom is found only in a surrendered life! Christian life is an exchanged life; His life for our life, His health for our sickness and His victories for our failures. Paul said in Galatians 2:20, "I have been crucified with Christ [that is, in Him I have shared His crucifixion]; it is no longer I who live, but Christ lives in me. The *life* I now live in the body I live by faith [by adhering to, relying on, and completely trusting] in the Son of God, who loved me and gave Himself up for me." This phrase "No longer I live yet I live" is a paradoxical truth that cannot be fully explained to the satisfaction of the carnal mind but can be experienced in this life.

Religion has defined surrendering to God as: putting on a low self-image, calling oneself an unworthy worm and constantly cry for God's mercy. When we do that and may be if God is in a good mood He will accept and love us. This may be an exaggeration, but many times that's been the tone of our surrender. This type of *surrender* is just asceticism in disguise. This is a work of the flesh, dressed up in religiously accepted terminology, and some churches are full of such delusional exhortations. You are even celebrated as a humble person for putting on such attitudes. The Apostle Paul called all such attitudes as self-imposed religion, false humility, but are of no value against the indulgence of the flesh (Col 2:23). Remember, you surrender your life either the religious way (work of the flesh) or God's way (walk of the spirit). There is no other option!

Biblical surrender is a two-way process. True biblical surrender is when we lay down our opinions and take up His opinions as truth, even if that doesn't make sense to our carnal minds[16]. For example, when you think and feel that you are a sinner but His word says that you are made righteous in Him, you have a choice. Either you go with your feelings and disregard what The Word says about you or surrender your opinions and feelings and accept God's view of you as truth. Walking by faith is not a blind leap into the dark. Walking by faith is to walk with your hearts fully persuaded by His promises because you have judged God faithful and that His promises are infallible.

Scripture Reference

1. When He had come down from the mountain, great multitudes followed Him. And behold, a leper came and worshiped Him, saying, "Lord, if You are willing, You can make me clean. Then Jesus put out His hand and touched him, saying, "I am willing; be cleansed." Immediately his leprosy was cleansed. Matthew 8:1-3, NKJV

2. God, who at various times and in various ways spoke in time past to the fathers by the prophets, has in these last days spoken to us by His Son, whom He has appointed heir of all things, through whom also He made the worlds. Hebrews 1:1-2, NKJV

3. And without controversy great is the mystery of godliness: God was manifested in the flesh, Justified in the Spirit, Seen by angels, Preached among the Gentiles, Believed on in the world, Received up in glory. 1 Timothy 3:16, NKJV

4. While he was still speaking, behold, a bright cloud overshadowed them; and suddenly a voice came out of the cloud, saying, "This is My beloved Son, in whom I am well pleased. Hear Him! Matthew 17:5, NKJV

5. And we know that the Son of God has come and has given us an understanding, that we may know Him who is true; and we are in Him who is true, in His Son Jesus Christ. This is the true God and eternal life. Little children, keep yourselves from idols. Amen. 1 John 5:20-21, NKJV

6. In the beginning was the Word, and the Word was with God, and the Word was God. He was in the beginning with God. All things were made through Him, and without Him nothing was made that was made. In Him was life, and the life was the light of men. John 1:1-4, NKJV

7. And the Word became flesh and dwelt among us, and we beheld His glory, the glory of the only begotten of the Father, full of grace and truth. John 1:14, NKJV

8. Now He did not do many mighty works there because of their unbelief. Matthew 13:58, NKJV

9. For this reason I also suffer these things; nevertheless I am not ashamed, for I know whom I have believed and am persuaded

that He is able to keep what I have committed to Him until that Day. 2 Timothy 1:12, NKJV

10. Surely He has borne our griefs. And carried our sorrows; Yet we [esteemed Him stricken, Smitten by God, and afflicted. But He was wounded for our transgressions, He was bruised for our iniquities; The chastisement for our peace was upon Him. And by His stripes we are healed. Isaiah 53:4-5, NKJV

11. For the mountains shall depart, and the hills be removed, But My kindness shall not depart from you, nor shall My covenant of peace be removed, Says the Lord, who has mercy on you. Isaiah 54:10, NKJV emphasis mine

12. Therefore, just as through one man sin entered the world, and death through sin, and thus death spread to all men, because all sinned—For until the law sin was in the world, but sin is not imputed when there is no law. Nevertheless death reigned from Adam to Moses, even over those who had not sinned according to the likeness of the transgression of Adam, who is a type of Him who was to come. Romans 5:12-14, NKJV

13. Christ has redeemed us from the curse of the law, having become a curse for us (for it is written, "Cursed is everyone who hangs on a tree") Galatians 3:13, NKJV

14. Then she came and worshiped Him, saying, "Lord, help me!" But He answered and said, "It is not good to take the children's bread and throw it to the little dogs." Matthew 15: 25-25, NKJV, emphasis mine

15. Then a certain scribe came and said to Him, "Teacher, I will follow You wherever You go." And Jesus said to him, "Foxes have holes and birds of the air have nests, but the Son of Man has nowhere to lay His head." Then another of His disciples said to Him, "Lord, let me first go and bury my father." But Jesus said to him, "Follow Me, and let the dead bury their own dead." Matthew 8:19-22, NKJV

16. But you have not so learned Christ, if indeed you have heard Him and have been taught by Him, as the truth is in Jesus: that you put off, concerning your former conduct, the old man which grows corrupt according to the deceitful lusts, and be renewed in the spirit of your mind, and that you put on the new man which was created according to God, in true righteousness and holiness. Ephesians 4:20-24, NKJV, emphasis mine

Chapter 2

THE KINGDOM OF GOD

The purpose Jesus came to earth is for the kingdom of God to be made accessible for ordinary men and women of all nations. The Bible says that God so loved the world that He gave his only begotten son that whosoever believes in Him should not perish but have eternal life[1]. In the Bible, the terms: the kingdom of God, Zion, eternal life, resurrected life, spirit life are all synonymous, and are interchangeably used. The Jews including the disciples who lived during the time of Jesus completely missed this purpose of Jesus. It's only after the disciples received the Holy Spirit their eyes were opened to this truth. The unbelieving Jews were looking for a glorious Messiah, an all-conquering king who would bring an external kingdom that will thwart all the other kingdoms of the earth and make Israel the global superpower or something along those lines. Their expectations were motivated by hatred towards Rome and other Gentile nations. After all, this is what is promised in the scriptures, according to their interpretation! They could not accept Jesus as the Messiah mostly because He did not fit their expectations. Ever since, the kingdom of God is misunderstood by many; in looking for an external kingdom, they missed what Jesus brought; an internal kingdom, a kingdom that will enter into the hearts of those who will put their faith in Him!

We see a glimpse of how this kingdom looks like in the book of Genesis. God created a garden and called it Eden. The Hebrew word for Eden means *house of pleasure*. The Garden of Eden was the home of Adam and it was a house of pleasure. Pleasure here means contentment. When the psalmist David said that there are pleasures in the right hand of God for evermore, he was talking about living a life of fulfilment and contentment. Sin in its core is the feeling of lack! The brief description of what is written about Eden throws some light into how life would have been for Adam in the garden. We can read about this in Genesis chapter 2. There is an unspoken tranquillity that transcends our inquisitive minds when we think about this garden. There were treasures of precious stones, fruit trees, flowering plants, vegetable gardens, provision, health, and prosperity for Adam to enjoy. All his needs were met in that garden. There was no sweat and no turmoil. Before the curse, there were no thorns or thistles growing on the Earth. It was too good to be true and yet that was the reality that Adam was created for.

THE KINGDOM LOST

When Adam sinned, God had to chase him out of the Garden of Eden. Adam's disobedience brought spiritual death. Sin is spiritual death, which means separation from God. Adam's disobedience is a result of a heart that moved from the place of faith to unbelief. Unbelief is the root of all sin!

Imagine a beautiful picture-perfect garden in your mind right now. Imagine that such a garden was present inside the heart of Adam. Remember, Adam's internal environment was an environment of peace and tranquillity. When spiritual death entered into him, that garden was corrupted and distorted with ghastly looking weeds, thorns, and thistles, metaphorically speaking. This was the state of Adam's heart after he sinned. An external perfect Garden called Eden now could not be the home of a man whose internal garden was corrupted with sin. This disharmony led God to chase him out of Eden. The Bible says the earth brought forth thorns and thistles which is now an earth that suits the internal condition of man's heart. The kingdom was lost both internally and externally. When sin brought curses on the earth, the external kingdom was lost forever. That is why we who are born again look forward to a new earth and a New Jerusalem where, righteousness dwells.[2]

In the Old Testament, God promised a restoration of this kingdom. This restoration is first and foremost an *internal restoration* that will usher in the external kingdom at the coming of our Lord Jesus Christ. But such knowledge is too profound for a mind that is only seeking God in the external reality and not inside the heart. *This is the essence of the legalistic mindset which is only interested in an outer change and not true life transformation.* The Jews both in the Old Testament and in the New Testament times were simply looking in the wrong places for the manifestation of the kingdom. Zion was also a reference to the kingdom of God in the Old Testament. Zion is first and foremost an internal kingdom[3]. Again, an externalist and legalistic mindset is looking for an external Zion. Yes, an external Zion is coming when Jesus comes in His Father's glory, in His second coming. But in fixating our minds on the external kingdom we are missing the glorious liberty of the internal Zion which is available for us, in the here and now.

In Isaiah, we see a description of this restoration which is first and foremost an internal restoration.

For the Lord will comfort Zion.

He will comfort all her waste places.

He will make her wilderness like Eden.

And her desert like the garden of the Lord.

Joy and gladness will be found in it,

Thanksgiving and the voice of melody.

Isaiah 51:3 NKJV

This is a beautiful picture of a heart that is healed of its maladies. This is precisely the picture Paul gave us about the life that is led by the spirit in the New Testament[4]. A spirit-led life is a life of joy and peace. The kingdom of God is righteousness, peace and joy in the Holy Spirit.

At the beginning of His earthly ministry, Jesus turned to the book of Isaiah and read the following passage,

The Spirit of the Lord *is* upon Me,

Because He has anointed Me

To preach the gospel to *the* poor;

He has sent Me to heal the broken-hearted,

To proclaim liberty to *the* captives

And recovery of sight to *the* blind,

To set at liberty those who are oppressed.

Luke 4:18 NKJV

Jesus proclaimed that His ministry was to preach a gospel that would bring healing to the hearts of man. Jesus preached about a kingdom that was about to come! Remember the heart of man is marred and broken by sin. You will understand more about the heart later. When the heart is healed, when eternal life enters into man, then there is gladness and thanksgiving with a voice of melody in the heart. It's almost impossible for a carnal externally focused mind to understand such a language. Jesus said that He will give peace, unlike the world gives[5]. The peace that the world

IT IS IN THE STATE OF PEACE, THE HUMAN BODY ENTERS INTO REST.

offers is based on circumstances. When all your bills are paid, when you are perfectly healthy, when all your relationships are working as it should be, you feel at peace. But Jesus offers a peace that transcends the natural mind and lifts one into a life that only those who have experienced can truly understand it. It's a peace, a tranquillity of mind that can be experienced but cannot be explained to the

53

satisfaction of a natural mind. Paul calls it: "A peace that passes all understanding"[6].

It is in this state of peace, the human body enters into a state of rest. Blood flows smoothly into all the organs of the body and immunity works harmoniously with the rest of the body. As you study further, you will see that this is what the life of God (eternal life) is capable of producing in you. It's not a mystical reality out there somewhere; it's at your reach inside you. Eternal life is now, the kingdom of God is within you, and as you understand the work of the Holy Spirit in you, you will understand that this is not a fantasy but a reality into which you can enter in this life.

THE KINGDOM WITHIN

When the Jews asked Jesus when the kingdom of God will come, Jesus answered them by saying, "The kingdom of God does not come with observation; nor will they say, see here, or see there. For the kingdom of God is within you.[7]" This was the mindset of the early Jews. This mindset was also seen among the disciples of the Lord Jesus. They asked a similar question to Jesus after

THE HOLY SPIRIT IS THE ONE WHO MAKES THIS REALM A VIBRANT REALITY.

the resurrection: "Lord, will you at this time restore the kingdom to Israel?"[8] They were still thinking about an external kingdom that will make Israel the superpower. Make no mistake, an external kingdom is coming! However, in keeping our minds focused on the external kingdom, we are missing the joyous life available in the internal kingdom of God. If I live the life that is now available in the kingdom of God in my spirit, my walk will be a walk of faith and love, and in doing that I will keep myself in the peace of God, following Him every day. So I will keep myself in the will of God, ready and prepared any time of the day to enter the external kingdom whenever that appears.

In His discourse about the kingdom of God, Jesus said to Nicodemus that unless one is born of water and of the spirit one cannot enter the kingdom of God[9]. At new birth, you received the kingdom of God inside you. However, one cannot experience this kingdom in day to day life unless he learns how to enter into it by the renewal of the mind. The Apostle Paul said that we experience transformation to the degree we renew our minds. As long as we fix our gaze externally there remains a veil in our heart[10]. But when one turns to the Lord, this veil is removed. You see, entering into the kingdom is not some magical, mystical formula one has to come up with. As the kingdom is already within you, you experience that kingdom by renewing your mind[11].

AT NEW BIRTH YOU RECEIVED THE KINGDOM OF GOD INSIDE YOU.

Before the crucifixion, Pilate asked Jesus if He was a King. Jesus answered Pilate and said that he was a King and His kingdom is unlike the earthly kingdoms[12]. The word *kingdom* in the original language could also be translated as a *realm*. The kingdom of God is the spiritual realm into which one is born into at the new birth. Before one is born again, he is a flesh being. As a flesh being, one has no access to the spiritual realities of God. The natural realm is the only reality in which he or she functions. The spiritual reality is oblivious to such a man. This realm is not accessible to the five senses[13]. It cannot be proved in a test tube or explained in such a way that makes perfect sense to a natural mind. But to those who are born again and want to follow Jesus as their Lord, this realm can be experienced in their hearts.

THE KING OF THE KINGDOM

Before Jesus ascended, He introduced the disciples to the Holy Spirit[14]. Throughout the life of Jesus, He addressed the Holy Spirit as the Father who lived inside Him and did all the works of God[15]. Jesus said to them that He would not leave them as orphans but would come to them[16]. The word orphan mean fatherless. The father He was talking about was the Holy Spirit which every born again believer could receive by faith. When the Holy Spirit comes to reside

THE HOLY SPIRIT WILL CAUSE YOU TO EXPERIENCE THE LIFE OF GOD WHICH IS INSIDE YOU.

inside a man, he has a Father, a King living inside him all the time. So the kingdom of God can also be understood as the Holy Spirit living inside us. This is the reason Paul said that the kingdom of God is righteousness, peace, and joy in the Holy Spirit[17].

The Holy Spirit is the one who makes this realm a vibrant reality in your heart. It's in the heart one experiences the kingdom. Faith springs out of a heart that believes in the word of God. When your mind is renewed to the word of God, you experience the truth of the word more real than what the five senses tell you. It is at this point, you enter into the kingdom. Kingdom living is not a mystical illusion as some have supposed to be. It's a realm into which one enters in his/her heart by faith through the renewing of the mind.

There is a picture described in the book of Isaiah, a garden transformed by the Holy Spirit. These are descriptions of the heart that is healed by the work of God.

Until the Spirit is poured upon us from on high.

And the wilderness becomes a fruitful field.

And the fruitful field is counted as a forest.

Isaiah 32:15 NKJV

My people will dwell in a peaceful habitation.

In secure dwellings and in quiet resting places.

Isaiah 32:18 NKJV

This is the life of peace Jesus came to give us. This is eternal life which is available for us now. The kingdom of God has entered into the hearts of men and women who have made Jesus their Lord. The Holy Spirit is our King and He desires to lead us into victory every day of our lives. He will cause you to experience outwardly the eternal life which is inside you. When your mind comes to harmony with your spirit (which has been infused with eternal life), you enter into a state of peace. Health and healing of your body and mind is a natural response to this life.

THE KINGDOM OF GOD AND THE WORD OF GOD

To explain the inner workings of the kingdom of God, Jesus used many parables. One such parable is the parable of the sower and the seed[18]. In this parable, the seed is the word and the ground is compared to the heart. The sower is the Son of God who went about sowing the seed of God's word into the hearts of the people. Many have intellectually pursued God's word but have not experienced the life of God's word. Many can quote and recite portions of scriptures but their lives are fraught with failures. I was one of those for several years. I have not arrived, however, by the grace of God; I left the place where I used to be!

GOD'S WORD WILL BRING SUCCESS IN EVERY AREA OF YOUR LIFE.

God's word will bring success in every area of your life. If it hasn't, it simply means that we have neglected the wisdom of Jesus' teachings. In the Lord's Prayer, Jesus taught His disciples to pray that men will experience heaven on earth as the kingdom came into the hearts of men[19]. This was not a novice idea Jesus brought by His teaching. Remember, all of Jesus' teachings are rooted in the Old Testament Scriptures. Jesus came to reveal how God's word would look like in real life when it is applied in your heart motivated by love. Jesus was bringing the secret wisdom that was hidden since the foundation of the world to light through simple life teachings[20].

58

Moses gave instructions to the children of Israel on how to conduct their lives in the Promised Land before his death. Listen carefully to his wisdom.

Therefore you shall lay up these words of mine in your heart and in your soul, and bind them as a sign on your hand and they shall be as frontlets between your eyes. You shall teach them to your children, speaking of them when you sit in your house, when you walk by the way, when you lie down and when you rise up. And you shall write them on the door post of your house and on your gates. That your days and the days of your children may be multiplied in the land of which the Lord swore to your fathers to give them, like the days of the heavens above the earth. Deuteronomy 11:18-21 NKJV

Both Jesus and Moses are on the same page. To experience heaven on earth, the wisdom is to keep the word of God in your heart. You will learn how to do this further along. The key to healing, health and abundant life which Jesus promised will become easy to your grasp as you understand your *heart* and learn how to keep God's word in your heart. The heart is the place where heaven's realities are experienced. When heaven invades your heart, then sickness will not be found in your heart. And when your heart is healed, your body will simply reflect this healing. It's that simple!

HEALING IN THE KINGDOM OF GOD

When you harmonize your mind to your born again spirit, you experience transformation. Transformation brings incredible benefits to your life. One of them is the healing of your body. Being spiritually minded is not being in the mystics but rather informing your mind with accurate information of what Christ has accomplished through His work on the cross. Again this is not mere mental information, but information that becomes revelation bringing transformation in your life. You will enter into what the Bible calls the *rest*. The writer of the book of Hebrews exhorts all believers to be diligent to enter that rest[21].

As your heart experiences healing and wholeness, then, and only then your external reality (body) will line up to the internal reality of your heart. Without a heart that has been made complete, all your attempts to change things in the external are only temporary. External modification is good but its hard work as it requires strong will power. This is the very deception of flesh. At any given time you are either walking in the spirit or walking in the flesh, there is no other option. The Bible calls walking in the spirit also as being spiritually-minded. Your mind dictates the conduct of your life. Your mind at any given time will be either under the control of the flesh or under the leadership of the spirit. Spirit-led life produces life and peace. Life includes health and healing! Wisdom says a *sound heart is life to the body (Proverbs 14:30a)*. This is not a metaphor, rather, a true statement.

A SOUND HEART IS LIFE TO THE BODY.

The light of the eyes rejoices the heart and a good report makes the bones healthy (Proverbs 15:30). The light of the eyes refers to where we focus our attention. The wisdom is to turn our focus from the external to the internal kingdom, the kingdom that is alive in our hearts!

Scripture Reference

1. For God so loved the world that He gave His only begotten Son, that whoever believes in Him should not perish but have everlasting life. John 3:16 NKJV
2. Now I saw a new heaven and a new earth, for the first heaven and the first earth had passed away. Also there was no more sea. Then I, John, saw the holy city, New Jerusalem, coming down out of heaven from God, prepared as a bride adorned for her husband. And I heard a loud voice from heaven saying, "Behold, the tabernacle of God is with men, and He will dwell with them, and they shall be His people. God Himself will be with them and be their God. Revelation 21: 1-3 NKJV *emphasis mine*
3. But you have come to Mount Zion and to the city of the living God, the heavenly Jerusalem, to an innumerable company of angels, to the general assembly and church of the firstborn who are registered in heaven, to God the Judge of all, to the spirits of just men made perfect, to Jesus the Mediator of the new covenant, and to the blood of sprinkling that speaks better things than that of Abel. Hebrews 12:22-24 NKJV
4. But the fruit of the Spirit is love, joy, peace, longsuffering, kindness, goodness, faithfulness, Galatians 5:22 NKJV
5. Peace I leave with you, My peace I give to you; not as the world gives do I give to you. Let not your heart be troubled, neither let it be afraid. John 14:27 NKJV
6. And the peace of God, which surpasses all understanding, will guard your hearts and minds through Christ Jesus. Philippians 4:7 NKJV
7. Now when He was asked by the Pharisees when the kingdom of God would come, He answered them and said, "The kingdom of God does not come with observation; nor will they say, 'See here!' or 'See there!' For indeed, the kingdom of God is within you." Luke 17:20-21 NKJV
8. Therefore, when they had come together, they asked Him, saying, "Lord, will you at this time restore the kingdom to Israel?" Acts 1:6 NKJV

9. Jesus answered, "Most assuredly, I say to you, unless one is born of water and the Spirit, he cannot enter the kingdom of God. John 3:5 NKJV

10. But even to this day, when Moses is read, a veil lies on their heart. 2 Corinthians 3:15 NKJV

11. And do not be conformed to this world, but be transformed by the renewing of your mind, that you may prove what is that good and acceptable and perfect will of God. Romans 12:2 NKJV

12. Jesus answered, "My kingdom is not of this world. If My kingdom were of this world, My servants would fight, so that I should not be delivered to the Jews; but now My kingdom is not from here." Pilate therefore said to Him, "Are You a king then?" Jesus answered, "You say rightly that I am a king. For this cause I was born, and for this cause I have come into the world, that I should bear witness to the truth. Everyone who is of the truth hears My voice." John 18:36-37 NKJV

13. The Spirit of truth, whom the world cannot receive, because it neither sees Him nor knows Him; but you know Him, for He dwells with you and will be in you. John 14:17 NKJV

14. And I will pray the Father, and He will give you another Helper, that He may abide with you forever. John 14:16 NKJV

15. Do you not believe that I am in the Father, and the Father in Me? The words that I speak to you I do not speak on My own authority; but the Father who dwells in Me does the works. John 14:19 NKJV

16. I will not leave you orphans; I will come to you. John 14:18 NKJV

17. For the kingdom of God is not eating and drinking, but righteousness and peace and joy in the Holy Spirit. Romans 14:17 NKJV

18. Listen! Behold, a sower went out to sow. Mark 4:3 NKJV

19. In this manner, therefore, pray Our Father in heaven. Hallowed be Your name. Your kingdom come. Your will be done. On earth as it is in heaven. Matthew 6:9-10 NKJV *emphasis mine.*

20. That it might be fulfilled which was spoken by the prophet, saying: "I will open My mouth in parables; I will utter things kept secret from the foundation of the world." Matthew 13:35 NKJV

21. Let us therefore be diligent to enter that rest, lest anyone fall according to the same example of disobedience. For the word of God *is* living and powerful, and sharper than any two-edged sword, piercing even to the division of soul and spirit, and of joints and marrow, and is a discerner of the thoughts and intents of the heart. Hebrews 4:11–12 NKJV

Chapter 3

JESUS THE SON OF GOD

The healing that you are keenly seeking begins with the revelation about Jesus the Son of God. Who is Jesus and what was His life purpose? As a young Christian growing up in church I have heard many preach about Jesus, that He came to die for the sins of mankind, if one believes in Him he or she will go to heaven or else will end up in hell. Many such things are preached in the name of the gospel, however, when I began to study the Bible to understand the gospel, I noted that the focus of the biblical gospel message was very different from what I heard in the church. First and foremost Jesus came to give us eternal life[1]. How you interpret *eternal life* could be the difference between experiencing God's quality of life now and just mundane boring powerless religious life? Jesus said that He came to give us life and have it in abundance. Many interpret that this abundant life is only available in the after-life. The truth is Jesus gives abundant life for us to experience now. Before we get to understand the abundant life, we need to understand the one who offers it.

To understand Jesus the Son of God we need to understand the creation of the first man. When Adam was created, his body was made from the earth and his spirit came from God[2]. Adam carried the image of God in his spirit; Adam was a spiritual being in an earthly body. Therefore, it was a perfectly healthy body that had not yet come under the power of spiritual death (sin). Adam was called the Son of God in the Bible[3]. In creation, Adam was God's kind. However, when he sinned, he fell from that glorious state. The man God originally

WHEN THE SPIRIT OF MAN WAS SEPARATED FROM GOD, MAN BECAME A FLESH BEING.

created was a *spirit-being* in a body but after the fall, Adam became a very different being and not the kind God created. God calls the fallen man as flesh[4]. When the spirit of man was separated from God, man became a flesh being living a life that was governed by the carnal mind. Before Adam fell, his mind was under the authority of his spirit. After he fell, his mind began to function independently of God. Satan now rules mankind through the mind that has not submitted to God[5].

THE SPIRIT SOUL & BODY OF JESUS (WHEN HE LIVED ON EARTH)

Every human being who came from Adam has the sin nature within him or her. The birth of Jesus was an extraordinary event in every sense and it is as supernatural as the creation of the first man in the Garden of Eden. Like how Adam was a prototype (the first of his kind), Jesus was also a prototype. The Son of God could not be born into the world by natural physical relationship. If Jesus was born by natural means, he would carry the sin nature in His spirit, as the seed would have come from an earthly father. With the birth of Jesus, a new type of man had come to live on the earth. A sinless spiritual man!

God sent the Word through the hands of the angel Gabriel to Mary[6]. When Mary received the Word, the Holy Spirit overshadowed her and Jesus was conceived in her womb[7]. The spirit of that child is none other than God's Word itself. In the beginning, was the Word, the Word was with God and now the Word has become flesh. God had manifested in the flesh[8]. Here flesh refers to the human body which was formed in Mary's womb. The Word literally became flesh[9]!

God in His wisdom chose a man called Abraham and out of this man God brought forth a group of people for Himself so that the Messiah could be brought into this world for mankind's redemption. The laws and the commandments, the atonement sacrifices, the priesthood, etc. that were given in the old covenant were given for this purpose. The purpose was to prepare that one person (Mary) who would step out in faith and would say yes to heaven's mandate. The Holy Spirit reveals this master plan through the writings of the Apostle Paul in the following scriptures.

For what then serveth the law? It was added because of transgressions until the Seed should come to whom the promise was made; and it was ordained by angels through the hand of a mediator. Galatians 3:19 NKJV

But when the fullness of the time had come, God sent forth His Son, **made of a woman**, made under the law. Galatians 4:4 NKJV emphasis mine

The Jesus who lived on the earth was the God-man. He was 100% God in his spirit and yet 100% man in His flesh. However, He was a spirit dominated man. In His spirit, He possessed the knowledge and wisdom of God. However, in His soul and body, He was like any other man who had to grow in wisdom and stature and favour with man[10]. His mind and body were a faculty of the earth but His spirit was a faculty of heaven. He was open to temptations like any other man. However, as a man who knew how to walk after His spirit, He overcame those temptations by yielding to the leadership of the spirit. The life of Jesus recorded in the four gospels is an example of how a life that is yielded to the Holy Spirit would look like for every born-again man and woman today. The flesh cannot be overcome by the flesh. The flesh can only be overcome by walking in the spirit[11]. Many religions around the world are trying to perfect man after the

> THE FLESH CAN ONLY BE OVERCOME BY WALKING IN THE SPIRIT.

flesh by beating the flesh with rules and legalistic rituals. This produces highly nervous, religious people and I was one of them for several years.

When Jesus was baptized in the River Jordan by John the Baptist, a voice came from heaven and made a startling declaration over Jesus, *"This is my beloved Son, in whom I am well pleased."* This declaration was made by the Father God over Jesus[12]. Up until that point, Jesus had not done any works of God: He had not preached a single sermon, not healed a single soul, and not raised any from the dead; nevertheless, Jesus was well pleased before the Father. Jesus was the pleasure of the Father! As born again men and women who are in union with Jesus in our spirit[13], we are the Father's pleasure. I believe this is the first declaration that God makes over us as soon as we make Jesus our Lord.

Many unaware of their position before their Father are nervously busy trying to please Him through religious duties. If you are born again you can rest because you are well pleased in your Father's eyes. This is your position in Christ. Your mind may disagree, your behaviour may not have come to line up with this truth yet, nevertheless, it's the way God sees you in Christ. The grace of God has made you and me as the Fathers' pleasure. When I got this revelation, I was so thrilled and I could not contain my joy. I walked about like a lost child having suddenly found his daddy in a crowd. A born again person becomes instantly the Father pleaser. You did not do one thing to attain this place, it was offered to you by grace and you accepted through faith in the finished work of Christ.

In summary, the spirit of Jesus is *The Word of God* which came from the Father but his body came from Mary. *Spirit (Word), soul and body!*

When Jesus received the baptism of the Holy Spirit, the Spirit took residence in Him from that day. In Christ, the Word and the Spirit came together from that day onwards.

The *spirit of Christ* as referred to in few places in the New Testament refers to the *word*[14]. At your new birth, it is the same word (spirit of Christ) united with your spirit and bought new birth!

When Jesus referred to Himself as the Son of God, the Pharisees and other unbelieving Jews picked up stones to stone Him[15]. They clearly understood that when one refers to himself as a son of God, he is making himself to be equal with God. This is one of the reasons they wanted Him crucified. Their accusation before Pilate was that Jesus called himself God[16]. Jesus made a true claim but the natural man could not accept His oneness with God. In their minds, it was a blasphemy. Like how Jesus was a Son of God, we too are sons and daughters of God in Him NOW!

SIN OFFERING

Jesus became a sin offering for the sins of the whole world. The Bible says, He who knew no sin became sin[17]! You need to grasp this truth. Sin refers to spiritual death. Jesus took on spiritual death on the cross. This is what it means; He became sin on the cross.

The entire human race who came from Adam inherited spiritual death from him. Remember, Adam was the prototype of mankind. When the master copy was corrupted, every subsequent copy that came from the master copy was also corrupted. Out of this spiritual death were birthed evil actions like adultery, theft, murder, etc. This works of darkness manifest itself

JESUS EXPERIENCED SPIRITUAL DEATH FIRST AND THEN PHYSICAL DEATH AT THE CROSS

as evil thoughts and evil behaviours over a spectrum. The depths of evil that we see in this world fall into this spectrum. You need to clearly understand that everyone is a sinner in Adam. It's not because you committed a sinful act that you became a sinner, rather, it's because you were a sinner in Adam you committed sinful actions. In the gospel message the early Apostles preached, they did not ask unsaved men to confess (behaviour) their sins to be saved, they simply asked them to believe in the Lord Jesus and confess Him as Lord[18].

When Jesus lived on the earth, He was the *only* sinless man! It was only at the cross Jesus became a perfect representation of the fallen man. When the Father withdrew His presence from Him, Jesus cried out, "My God, My God why have you forsaken me"[19]. It is at this point He took on the nature of fallen man. It is at the cross Jesus experienced spiritual death and died in the spirit first. It is at this point He became the perfect representation of the whole fallen human race. The Apostle Paul said it this way; "When one died for all, then all died[20]." Jesus became the last man of the

Adamic race. In the book of Corinthians, one of the names of Jesus was called the last Adam[21]. Meaning, after Him there is not going to be another Adam. In the risen Christ, the Adamic race ceases to exist and a new race is birthed. This is called the new creation or new creature depending on which translation of the Bible you are reading.

Jesus prophesied that He would spend three days and three nights in the heart of the earth like how the prophet Jonah spent three days and three nights in the belly of the whale[22]. In the book of Jonah chapter 2, Jonah prays a prophetic prayer from the belly of the whale. This is a type of prayer Jesus prayed from Hades. The heart of the earth is a reference to Hades. It is the place where the unsaved dead go. Jesus was under condemnation

JESUS WAS UNDER CONDEMNATION AND JUDGMENT FOR THE SIN OF MANKIND.

and judgment for the sins of mankind. Jesus was paying the full price of the first man's sin. The disciples who were standing at the foot of the cross and looking at the death of Jesus were oblivious to what was happening to Him. This revelation was hidden from them at that point in time. The sufferings of the Messiah as a sin offering were seen by many Old Testament prophets including David. David wrote about this quite vividly in Psalm 22. David, who was seeing in the realm of the spirit, saw the Messiah coming under the power of Satan and his forces. Those three days were the darkest days of human history. Satan had finally found the seed which he was searching for generations since the time of

Cain and Abel. For three days every demon would have celebrated the victory of darkness over the light in Hades. Little did they know the plan of God about the resurrection. Had they known they would not have killed the Lord of Glory!

RESURRECTION POWER & RIGHTEOUSNESS

After those three dark days, God the Father declared that the penalty for sin was paid in full and He sent the Holy Spirit to raise Jesus up from Hades. Every demon would have quivered in fear when Jesus Christ was revived and resurrected by the Holy Spirit. The resurrected spirit of Jesus entered the body which was in the tomb and His body was vitalized by the born-again spirit. Every demon knew what this meant. This is the end of spiritual death! This is the end of demonic oppression of mankind! Remember, the man was under the oppression of the spirit of this world, the ruler of darkness. Satan ruled

> **AT THE RESURRECTION, JESUS BECAME THE FIRST FRUIT OF A NEW KIND OF MAN.**

the world through the mind (flesh) of spiritually dead men. Spiritually dead men had no power over darkness. They were slaves of sin. However, everything was changed at the resurrection of Jesus. Christ's resurrection means the end of demonic reign over mankind. This is the end of Satan's rule by force. He still rules through deception. However, his absolute power over mankind was broken. Through death (spiritual), Jesus paralyzed Satan who had power over death (spiritual)[23].

Jesus became the first begotten son at resurrection[24,25]. You need to understand the difference between the *only begotten Son* and the *first begotten Son*. During His earthly life, Jesus was the only begotten Son of the Father. But at the cross, He became like any other sinful man. It was at the resurrection from the dead, He became the FIRST begotten of the Father[26]. The word begotten means to give birth or offspring. At His birth, Jesus was the only offspring of the Father. At the resurrection, Jesus became the first offspring of the Father. Meaning, everyone who chooses to put their faith in Jesus is going to be the subsequent offspring of the Father. If you are born again, you are God's offspring! You have been elevated to the position of God's kind[27].

A MAN (JESUS CHRIST) HAS OVERCOME SATAN AND UTTERLY ANNIHILATED HIS POWERS

At the resurrection, Jesus became the first fruit of a new kind of man. The provision for the termination of the Adamic race is paved through the work of the cross. In Christ, a new breed of creation is wrought. This is why Paul says if any man is in Christ, he is a new creation. All the authority that was lost by Adam at the Garden of Eden was also regained. Jesus proclaims after His resurrection that all authority has been given to Him in heaven and on earth[28]. His name sends shivers to the demonic world. He had been there, defeated them on their turf and now has come alive. Had the demons known this marvellous work of God, they would not have crucified the Lord of Glory! [29]

Jesus paraded the demonic forces in Hades. He made a public spectacle of them[30]. I can almost see in my heart how all the saints who were watching this scene must have been shouting in jubilation. A man (Adam) plunged us all into sin. A man (Jesus Christ) has overcome Satan and utterly annihilated his powers and delivered us from the clutches of sin. Every angel must have gone into a frenzy of rapturous applause at the conquest of satanic forces by a single man. Jesus did it all single-handed. There was a shout in heaven at that time, who is this King of Glory? The Lord mighty in battle![30]

At the cross, when the Father withdrew the Holy Spirit, Jesus was made sin and then at the resurrection, Jesus was made righteous again. Righteousness was lost for a brief period time (3 days & 3 nights), but righteousness was restored in the spirit at His resurrection. This righteousness is no ordinary righteousness; it's a righteousness that defeated Satan. A child of God is made righteous with this righteousness. On the day you discover this marvellous revelation, every demon that has been oppressing you will simply scoot for their lives. They don't want you to know this truth. Now that you do, they have lost their powers over you. They have been lying to you all these days. When you come to understand this marvellous revelation, you will cast demons out like how one of the mighty men of David chased their enemies[32]. King David had a band of mighty men around him. Their bravery acts recorded in the scriptures are pictures of what every child of God can do to the demonic forces. Under the old covenant, they were masters over their enemies. How much more under the new covenant can you and I become masters over our oppressors? Just think about that!

When the Father sees you, He sees His righteousness over you, a righteousness that conquered every demon, every sickness, and poverty[33]. The very righteousness of Jesus is what you are clothed with. When you get the revelation of this righteousness: that will be the end of sin problem and the end of talk of weakness. He has become your strength now. It's the end of sickness, why? Because He became your disease on the cross! It's the end of poverty, why? Because He took your poverty upon Himself[34]. It's the end of destructive addictions, why? Because His righteousness breaks the backbone of sinful habits.

The Hebrew meaning for the word righteousness means *to be made as you should be*. You are made as you should be in your *spirit* before the Father. No remembrance of sin! You are before the Father as Jesus stood before the Father during His earthly walk. When you fully understand this revelation, you will stop viewing yourself as a sinner. When you see this clearly in your heart, His resurrection becomes your resurrection. This is what it means to believe in your heart that God raised Jesus Christ from the dead[35].

Now you know who the Son of God is and the power behind that name Jesus. This is the beginning of your healing journey!

Scripture Reference

1. The thief does not come except to steal, and to kill, and to destroy. I have come that they may have life, and that they may have it more abundantly. John 10:10 NKJV
2. And the Lord God formed man of the dust of the ground, and breathed into his nostrils the breath of life; and man became a living being. Genesis 2:7 NKJV
3. The son of Enosh, the son of Seth, the son of Adam, the son of God. Luke 3:38 NKJV
4. And the Lord said, "My Spirit shall not strive with man forever, for he is indeed flesh; yet his days shall be one hundred and twenty years." Genesis 6:3 NKJV
5. And you He made alive, who were dead in trespasses and sins, in which you once walked according to the course of this world, according to the prince of the power of the air, the spirit who now works in the sons of disobedience, among whom also we all once conducted ourselves in the lusts of our flesh, fulfilling the desires of the flesh and of the mind, and were by nature children of wrath, just as the others. Ephesians 3:1-3 NKJV
6. Now in the sixth month the angel Gabriel was sent by God to a city of Galilee named Nazareth, to a virgin betrothed to a man whose name was Joseph, of the house of David. The virgin's name was Mary. Luke 1:26-27 NKJV
7. Then Mary said, "Behold the maidservant of the Lord! Let it be to me according to your word." And the angel departed from her. Luke 1:38 NKJV
8. In the beginning was the Word, and the Word was with God, and the Word was God. He was in the beginning with God. All things were made through Him, and without Him nothing was made that was made. John 1:1-3 NKJV
9. And the Word became flesh and dwelt among us, and we beheld His glory, the glory as of the only begotten of the Father, full of grace and truth. John 1:14 NKJV
10. And the Child grew and became strong in spirit, filled with wisdom; and the grace of God was upon Him. Luke 2:40 NKJV

11. I say then: Walk in the Spirit, and you shall not fulfill the lust of the flesh. Galatians 5:16 NKJV

12. And suddenly a voice came from heaven, saying, "This is My beloved Son, in whom I am well pleased." Matthew 3:17 NKJV

13. But he who is joined to the Lord is one spirit with Him. 1 Corinthians 6:17 NKJV

14. But you are not in the flesh but in the Spirit, if indeed the Spirit of God dwells in you. Now if anyone does not have the Spirit of Christ, he is not His. Romans 8:9 NKJV emphasis mine.

15. But Jesus answered them, "My Father has been working until now, and I have been working." Therefore the Jews sought all the more to kill Him, because He not only broke the Sabbath, but also said that God was His Father, making Himself equal with God. John 7:17-18 NKJV

16. The Jews answered him, "We have a law, and according to our law He ought to die, because He made Himself the Son of God." John 19:7 NKJV

17. For He made Him who knew no sin to be sin for us, that we might become the righteousness of God in Him. 2 Corinthians 5:21 NKJV

18. So they said, "Believe on the Lord Jesus Christ, and you will be saved, you and your household." Acts 16:31 NKJV

19. And about the ninth hour Jesus cried out with a loud voice, saying, "Eli, Eli, lama sabachthani?" that is, "My God, My God, why have You forsaken Me?" Matthew 27:46 NKJV

20. For the love of Christ compels us, because we judge thus: that if One died for all, then all died. 2 Corinthians 5:14 NKJV

21. And so it is written, "The first man Adam became a living being." The last Adam became a life-giving spirit. 1Corinthians 15:45 NKJV

22. For as Jonah was three days and three nights in the belly of the great fish, so will the Son of Man be three days and three nights in the heart of the earth. Matthew 12:40 NKJV

23. Inasmuch then as the children have partaken of flesh and blood, He Himself likewise shared in the same, that through death He might destroy him who had the power of death, that is, the devil. Hebrews 2:14 NKJV

24. So also Christ did not glorify Himself to become High Priest, but it was He who said to Him: "You are My Son, Today I have begotten You." Hebrews 5:5 NKJV

25. God has fulfilled this for us their children, in that He has raised up Jesus. As it is also written in the second Psalm: "'You are My Son, Today I have begotten You.' Actus 13:33 NKJV

26. And He is the head of the body, the church, who is the beginning, the firstborn from the dead, that in all things He may have the pre-eminence. Colossians 1:18 NKJV

27. Whoever believes that Jesus is the Christ is born of God, and everyone who loves Him who begot also loves him who is begotten of Him. 1 John 5:1 NKJV

28. And Jesus came and spoke to them, saying, "All authority has been given to Me in heaven and on earth. Matthew 28:18 NKJV

29. Which none of the rulers of this age knew; for had they known, they would not have crucified the Lord of glory. 1 Corinthians 2:8 NKJV

30. The bond, with its requirements, which was in force against us and was hostile to us, He cancelled, and cleared it out of the way, nailing to His cross. And the hostile princes and rulers He shook off from Himself, and boldly displayed them as His conquests, when by the Cross He triumphed over them. Colossians 2:14-5 Weymouth Translation

31. Who is this King of glory? The Lord strong and mighty, The Lord mighty in battle. Psalm 24:8 NKJV

32. David's mighty men. 2 Samuel 23:8-39

33. You are of God, little children, and have overcome them, because He who is in you is greater than he who is in the world. 1 John 4:4 NKJV

34. For you know the grace of our Lord Jesus Christ, that though He was rich, yet for your sakes He became poor, that you through His poverty might become rich. 2 Corinthians 8:9 NKJV

35. That if you confess with your mouth the Lord Jesus and believe in your heart that God has raised Him from the dead, you will be saved. Romans 10:9 NKJV.

Chapter 4

NEW BIRTH

In my view, the most hidden truth about a born again Christian is the truth about *New Birth*. What really happened to a person when he or she was born again? What did the Apostle Paul mean by *we are a new creation in Christ?*[1]

I gave my life to Jesus and became a *born again* Christian at the age of 17. For several years, nearly 20, I never understood what really had happened inside my heart. This ignorance kept me in bondage to sin, sickness, disease and a poverty mindset. This is mainly because I wasn't renewing my mind according to the word of God. Also, sadly, such knowledge is not widely taught from the pulpit.

My goal is to get my body and mind healed and why do I need to know about the new birth, you may wonder? Trust me, your healing is intricately woven in your new identity as you are about to find out.

Paul said that when one believes in his or her heart that God raised Jesus from the dead and confesses with his or her mouth the Lordship of Jesus, one is born again[2]. To believe means to see and perceive with your deep thoughts.

> **TO BELIEVE MEANS TO SEE AND PERCEIVE WITH YOUR DEEP THOUGHTS.**

To say that I believe in the resurrection of Jesus is to say that I see His resurrection in my heart. At the point of you seeing this, His resurrection becomes your resurrection in your heart. You are now raised together with Him![3] Since your heart is the seat of your true identity; when you believe that Jesus was raised in your heart, His resurrection becomes your identity. This is what Paul meant when he said "He is your life!" in the book of Colossians[4].

A GRAIN OF WHEAT

Once, a group of Greeks wanted to see Jesus. They went to His disciples Andrew and Philip, who in turn took them to meet Jesus. Now, follow this conversation between them carefully.

> Now there were certain Greeks among those who came up to worship at the feast. Then they came to Philip,

who was from Bethsaida of Galilee, and asked him, saying, "Sir, we wish to see Jesus."

Philip came and told Andrew, and in turn Andrew and Philip told Jesus.

But Jesus answered them, saying, "The hour has come that the Son of Man should be glorified. Most assuredly, I say to you, unless a grain of wheat falls into the ground and dies, it remains alone; but if it dies, it produces much grain. He who loves his life will lose it, and he who hates his life in this world will keep it for eternal life. John 12:20-24 NKJV

(If you skim through this conversation superficially, you will probably miss the wisdom from the master.)

All they wanted was to see Jesus, for which Jesus could have replied, "Here I am." But that's not how Jesus answered them. For a long time His answer troubled me. One day, I finally saw what Jesus was saying, and it is marvellous!

The Greeks are philosophical and intellectual people. In the Bible, the Greeks are often a picture of someone who is seeking the pursuit of intellectual knowledge. They are people driven by *mental activity,* very much like the people of the 21st century today.

Jesus speaks about a kernel of wheat. If you plant one grain of wheat on the ground, a crop will come out of it and from that crop numerous kernels of wheat can be harvested. However, if the grain of wheat is not planted in the ground, it will just stay single. The kernel of wheat is the life of Jesus. If Jesus didn't go to the cross to die, He will remain alone. But if He died and is raised again, His resurrection will pave the way for the resurrection of many millions of people. Then these millions of people will see Him in their own hearts. Jesus was pointing out to them that the only way to truly see Him is, to see in their hearts and not in their intellectual minds.

To love your life means to hold onto life the way you have come to understand it through the knowledge of the world system. Jesus is asking you to let go of that life and grab hold of His life which is inside you, in your heart.

Today, we can see Jesus! He always meets us in the place where God said he would meet man, which is in the garden of our heart. In the book of Revelation, we read about Jesus standing at the door and knocking[5]. For an unbeliever, He is knocking at the door from the outside. But for a born again believer, Jesus is knocking at the door of the heart from the inside. Will you respond and enter into communion with Him in your heart or will you just be driven by your mind and intellectual pursuit of God?

NEW BIRTH

I want to show you from the scriptures how this new birth actually happens, so that you will come to accurately understand your true identity. You may want to read this slowly and carefully!

We were saved by Grace through faith[6]. The faith to be saved came in the gospel which you heard at the beginning. You heard about Jesus, you probably did not hear a lot of details, nevertheless, you saw the need for Him in your life and you said *yes to Him*. The Spirit of God was graciously wooing you into the presence of God. Right at that time, the miracle of new birth burst in your heart! You probably didn't understand why suddenly you felt joy and light in your heart. The degree of this experience is subjective and varied. Nevertheless, you experienced something which you couldn't explain. You were born again from above! [7]

You stood there hearing the gospel message preached to you. Packed inside the gospel message was the living word of God (spirit of Christ). Remember, from the previous chapter, I showed you that the *spirit of Christ* is another term for *the word*. For now, let's keep the term *spirit of Christ* as separate from the *Holy Spirit*. In the grand scheme

THE "WORD" JOINED WITH YOUR SPIRIT AT NEW BIRTH.

of truth; God the Father, the Word, and the Holy Spirit all are one and the same. For now, let's see them as separate for us to grasp the inner workings of the new birth.

When you responded positively to the gospel, the word of God (spirit of Christ) joined with your spirit and brought life and immortality to your spirit man[8]. Paul said you were raised together with Him. The Greek word used for 'together with' is a medical term. That word is *suzoopoieo*. This word means 'to resuscitate in combination with.'[9]

I have provided CPR (cardiopulmonary resuscitation) to many patients in my career. In CPR, we resuscitate and restart the heart and keep the blood flowing to the brain by external chest compressions. On the contrary, God resuscitated us by an internal work, by uniting His word (spirit of Christ) and our spirit together. This happened on that day when you responded to the gospel and this union is inseparable. This happened inside you, in your spirit! He who is joined to the Lord is one spirit with Him says the Bible[10]. The Greek word used for 'one' is *heis*. This word means a *numerical one* and not *two appearing as one*. The spirit of Christ (word of God) and our dead spirit joined together and became ONE. You are alive to God in the spirit. You are immortal in your spirit.

HE WHO JOINED WITH THE LORD IS ONE SPIRIT WITH HIM.

You were translated from the kingdom of darkness into the kingdom of His son of His love[11]. Your spirit is full of light! This is what it means when God said, "I will put My laws in their mind and write them on their hearts; and I will be their God, and they shall be My people" (Hebrews 8:10). The *mind* here refers to the deep thoughts of your heart and not the intellectual mind. The spirit part of your heart has been completely renewed. God's word is written in your spirit and therefore the spirit communicates through intuitive knowledge.

THE WORD OF GOD

The word of God is permanently written in the spirit part of your heart. James calls it the *implanted word* [12]. The word has been implanted in your spirit!

Therefore lay aside all filthiness and overflow of wickedness, and receive with meekness the **implanted word,** which is able to save your souls.

But be doers of the word, and not hearers only, deceiving yourselves. For if anyone is a hearer of the word and not a doer, he is like a man observing his natural face in a mirror; for he observes himself, goes away, and immediately forgets what kind of man he was. But he who looks into the perfect law of liberty and continues in it, and is not a forgetful hearer but a doer of the work, this one will be blessed in what he does. James 1:21–25 NKJV emphasis mine

Therefore, James is calling believers everywhere to receive the implanted word, meaning, to renew their intellectual minds by seeing the reflection of their spirit in the law of liberty[13]. Remember, a mirror only reflects what is in front of it. Likewise, the Bible is a book that reflects what is in your spirit, showing your true identity. This is the wisdom James is giving to his listeners. This is also the reason why you should read the Bible, to see your reflection! Your true identity!

The Apostle Peter said that we were born again by the incorruptible seed of God's word and he quoted a scripture from the book of Isaiah. Again, I want you to see this truth from the epistle of Peter.

Since you have purified your souls in obeying the truth through the Spirit in sincere love of the brethren, love one another fervently with a pure heart, having been born again, not of corruptible seed but incorruptible, through the word of God which lives and abides forever, because

"All flesh is as grass, And all the glory of man as the

flower of the grass. The grass withers, And its flower falls away, But the word of the Lord endures forever." Now this is the word which by the gospel was preached to you. 1 Peter 1:20-24 NKJV

Look at the last statement Peter made; "This is the word which by the gospel came to you." The living word (spirit of Christ) was hidden in the gospel message and you were made alive by the spirit of Christ (Word).

Here is the main essence of what I am saying,

- ❖ The Old Testament is the revelation that God is The Word
- ❖ The four Gospels are the revelation; the Word came in the flesh.
- ❖ The Apostle's epistles are the revelation that now we are the word in the flesh. Your true identity is the word!

Since you are the offspring of God (who is the Word), you are also the word in the flesh.

Now, look at what the Apostle John wrote about our identity in his epistle.

Brethren, I write no new commandment to you, but an old commandment which you have had from the beginning. **The old commandment is the word** which you heard from the beginning. Again, a new commandment I write to you, **which thing is true in Him and in you,** because the darkness is passing away, and the true light is already shining. 1 John 2:7-8NKJV emphasis mine

What was true in Him? The word! Now the same is true in you! Do you see it now? This is the reason that every born again Christian longs for God's word deep in the inside. You are a child of the word. You are at home when you arrive at the word. Your life is intricately woven in the fabric of God's word. You are wired to live by every word that proceeds from God's mouth. Your heart is beating faster even as you read this. The Holy Spirit is bearing witness inside you concerning this truth. You probably have been waiting to hear this truth all your life. Now, joy unspeakable is flowing in your heart. In the subsequent chapters, you will learn what the practical application of this revelation is.

God's report is the only report that is true of you. Every other report is only describing your external reality. God's word is describing your true reality which is your spirit. Now, do you understand why you should read the Bible? You search the Bible to understand who you truly are in Him. Jesus said that the branch that does not abide in the vine will wither away. Likewise, if we do not renew our mind to who we are in the spirit, we will not experience the life of the spirit in our day to day life.

Now, you can understand the language of the Apostles when they said, "You are of God, little children[14]," "He who believes Jesus as the Christ is born of God.[15]" Such language eluded you all these years. Not anymore! Now search through the scriptures like a treasure hunter seeking for those words that describe you. Now that you understand this, you clearly see the value of renewing your mind to the truth.

A WORD ABOUT THE TRUTH

The word truth means reality. Your mind receives information that comes from different sources. That information may be factual or fake news. That information may be from the Bible or the news media. Remember, God's word is the truth but it only comes *as information*. It becomes reality in your heart through meditation, then, only then that information has become *truth to you*. Until then, it's only information! You can quote it, recite it, memorize it, sing about it, but it's not truth in your heart! Your heart is the place where realities are born. Once formed, you live by those realities. You may not be conscious of this inner working; nevertheless, they dictate the conduct of your life. This is what it means in the Bible; "As a man thinketh in his heart so is he.[23]" You are living by the realities which you have created all your life. Remember, only you have the power to create realities pertaining to your life. Every information you receive daily has the potential to become a reality through your consent and choice. This is the reason why wisdom cries out to guard your heart with all diligence for out of the heart springs the issues of life (Proverbs 4:23). The word *issue* here also means *boundary*. So we have an invisible boundary inside our hearts and we are only comfortable living within that boundary. These boundaries are erected by the beliefs of our heart. The only way to expand our life boundary is to change the beliefs of our

GOD'S REPORT IS THE ONLY REPORT THAT IS TRUE OF YOU.

heart.

NEW CREATION

The church in Corinth had many internal issues. Paul, coming to know about those issues, addressed them by writing two letters. In the first epistle, he expressed his displeasure with them for creating divisions in the church[17]. By doing this, he said, they were acting like *mere men*. They left their walk in the spirit and now behaving like carnal men.

> For you are still carnal. For where there are envy, strife, and divisions among you, are you not carnal and behaving like mere men? For when one says, "I am of Paul," and another, "I am of Apollos," are you not carnal? 1 Corinthians 3: 3–4 NKJV

The Greek word he used for *men* is 'anthropos' which means *human being*. Paul makes quite a statement! He tells the Corinthian born again believers that they were behaving like *human beings*. So, who were they in actuality? If they were acting like mere human beings, the notion is that they are not mere human beings then. Were they? They are born again men! Spirit-filled men! God

EVERY BORN AGAIN CHRISTIAN IS GOD'S ETERNAL LIFE IN A HUMAN BODY

inside men! Covenant men! If you are born again, then you too are not just mere human beings. You have been lifted from the place of weakness to the place of His strength. You are seated together with Him!

Paul calls believers as new creations! This is a new type of creation that never existed before. With the resurrection of Christ, the Adamic race ceased to exist in Him. Christ was called the last Adam! A born again Christian is God's eternal life in a human body. A new kind of man! Now imagine if this truth was realized and actuated by every believer. What kind of people we will be? Every demon knows who we are in Christ; every Angelic being knows who we are in Christ. But it's of no use until you and I realize who we are in Christ and start acting that way.

Every writer in the New Testament is calling believers everywhere to come to this realization and align their outward behaviour to who they already are in the spirit. This is what it means to walk in the spirit! Without walking in the spirit we will not experience the resurrected life in health.

The word fellowship means to share, exchange or joint participation. God is faithful and He is calling us to share or jointly participate with the resurrected life of Jesus which is inside our spirit[18]. When you come to embrace this truth in your mind, your weak and beggarly prayer life is over. You will walk and talk like mature sons of God. The Apostle Paul said that the whole creation is yearning for the revelation of such sons and daughters of God[19]. The word "sons" here means a mature son of God who knows his position in Christ and he is acting that way.

Your attitude toward sickness and pain in your body will change when you wrap yourself (thoughts and emotions) around the implanted resurrected life. This is the point where your experience of divine healing leaps to another level.

ONE DIED FOR ALL THEN ALL DIED

For the love of Christ compels us, because we judge thus: that **if One died for all, then all died; and He died for all**, that those who live should live no longer for themselves, but for Him who died for them and rose again. 2 Corinthians 5: 14-15 NKJV emphasis mine

In Adam, the entire human race was dead i.e. separated from God. Spiritual death means separation from the Father. When Christ came into the earth, He was the only man alive in the spirit. He walked among spiritually dead men. They could not be born again as Christ had not yet gone to the cross. No one could be born again until Christ rose from the dead. When Christ died on the cross, He took on our death i.e. spiritual death on Himself. By doing so, He became one of us! He became the perfect representation of all dead men on the cross. It was our spiritual death that was placed on Him. The whole dead human race was perfectly represented on the cross. This is the substitutionary death of Jesus Christ. Substitution means a perfect sinless man who took on the sin of those whom he represented.

ON ACCOUNT OF JESUS YOU ARE QUALIFIED TO CLAIM EVERY PROMISE IN THE BIBLE.

(I am aware of some false doctrines which say that in Adam all died and in Christ, all human beings are **saved.**

This is an erroneous doctrine and this is not what the Bible, nor the Apostle Paul, nor am I trying to say here.)

We all came from Adam. So when he sinned, we all sinned in him. In Adam, we did not have a choice. When Christ was crucified on the cross, the whole world was crucified on the cross, so to speak. This is what Paul means by *when one died for all, then all died.* However, Christ was raised from the dead. Therefore, whosoever choses to believe the resurrection of Christ in their hearts, they are counted as raised together with Him. When Christ rose from the dead, the choice was restored to mankind. Now, spiritually dead men can call upon Him and be born again. When we do that, His resurrected life becomes our life! Remember, the choice to make Him the Lord is ours, only ours! Now, we don't look at ourselves, rather; we look to him to understand our life. Paul explains this paradox beautifully in the following verse,

THE INHERITANCE WE HAVE IN THE NEW COVENANT ARE THE PROMISES OF GOD

> **I have been crucified with Christ**; it is no longer I who live, but Christ lives in me; and **the *life* which I now live** in the flesh **I live by faith in the Son of God**, who loved me and gave Himself for me. Galatians 2:20 NKJV

You see, there are only two kinds of men living on earth today. One group (church) is alive in Christ by placing their faith in the risen Lord, and the rest are dead. Spiritually dead people will not enter into heaven. Only those who are alive in Christ will be entering into heaven.

NEW COVENANT

The new covenant is the only covenant that is very different from every other covenant God made with man. In the new covenant, God made a new type of covenant because of the resurrection of Jesus. *The new covenant was not made between God and individual believers.* It was made between God and the man Jesus Christ. Paul made it clear that the promise was made to Abraham and to his seed[20]. Not seeds as in many! When Jesus rose from the dead, He inherited all the promises of God. Therefore, all the promises of God were yes and Amen in Jesus Christ[21]. God's goodness towards us no longer depends on our thimble promises we make to Him, rather, it is now based on the resurrection of Jesus. It is by these promises that we participate in the divine nature which is in our spirit[22]. When you place your faith in Jesus, you are baptized or immersed into the body of Jesus. Paul said that those who are baptized into Christ have put on Christ. On account of Jesus, you are qualified to claim every promise in the Bible because Jesus inherited all the promises and you are in Him. No matter to whom the promise was made both in the Old and the New Testaments, they are ours by faith in Jesus. In Christ, we are Abraham's seed[23]. Therefore, we can boldly enter God's presence and actuate any promise that caters to our needs. As we learn to partake of His promises, we get to enjoy this inheritance which produces health and healing in every area of our lives. If you did not understand this covenant, Satan will deceive you, showing your faults, and then you disqualify yourself and miss out on God. As soon as you have placed your eyes on your works, good or bad, you have removed your eyes from Jesus. You become sin conscious and you disqualify yourself. This is the root of condemnation. As soon as condemnation enters your heart, you disqualify yourself from enjoying the benefits of God. Therefore, let us run with our eyes looking unto Jesus[24].

OLD MAN: DEAD OR ALIVE?

Therefore, if anyone is in Christ, he is a new creation; **old things have passed away; behold, all things have become new. Now all things are of God**, who has reconciled us to Himself through Jesus Christ, and has given us the ministry of reconciliation 2 Corinthians 5:17-18 NKJV emphasis mine

Let us examine this scripture one more time! If any man is in Christ, he is a new man! The old man is gone and in his place, the new man has come. Many have not understood this and they are trying to crucify the old man. Your old man, that dead spirit is gone. He was buried with Jesus at His death and burial. Paul said, "Therefore we were buried with Him through baptism into death, that just as Christ was raised from the dead by the glory of the Father, even so we also should walk in newness of life. For if we have been united together in the likeness of His death, certainly we also shall

WE PROCLAIM THE LORD'S DEATH WHEN WE PARTAKE IN COMMUNION.

be in the likeness of His resurrection, knowing this, that our old man was crucified with Him, that the body of sin might be done away with, that we should no longer be slaves of sin (Romans 6:5–6)." The words *planted together* means inseparable union. Then why did Paul say that you should put off the old man in another place, you may ask? Let's examine that scripture closely.

That you put off, concerning your **former conduct, the old man** which grows corrupt according to the deceitful lusts, and be renewed in the spirit of your mind, and that you put on the new man which was created according to God, in true righteousness and holiness. Ephesian 4:22-25 NKJV emphasis mine.

The Apostle Paul is actually referring to the *former conduct of the Old man* and *not the old man* as such. Can you see it? Before you were born again, your old man has trained your mind to think and act a certain way, so to speak. Now, that old man is gone, Paul is urging believers to re-educate (renew) their minds and constantly put on the new man. Put-off and put-on is a spiritual exercise that we shall learn in the chapter on meditation. Also note, Paul is not asking to become righteous. He is urging the believers to put on the new man who is already made righteous and holy in Christ. If you think you need to become righteous by good works, you are denying the work of Jesus on the cross.

The old man was the life source of your sickness and disease. Now that the axe has been laid at the roots of your sickness and disease, they have lost its power. Paul said that we proclaim the Lord's death when we partake in communion. Now, we understand what that means. We remind ourselves of our death in His death by proclaiming the death of our Lord when we take communion.

Scripture Reference

1. Therefore, if anyone *is* in Christ, *he is* a new creation; old things have passed away; behold, all things have become new. 2 Corinthians 5:17 NKJV
2. That if you confess with your mouth the Lord Jesus and believe in your heart that God has raised Him from the dead, you will be saved. Romans 10:9 NKJV
3. Even when we were dead in trespasses, made us alive together with Christ (by grace you have been saved), [6] and raised *us* up together, and made *us* sit together in the heavenly *places* in Christ Jesus. Ephesians 2:5-6 NKJV
4. When Christ *who is* our life appears, then you also will appear with Him in glory. Colossians 3:4 NKJV
5. Behold, I stand at the door and knock. If anyone hears My voice and opens the door, I will come in to him and dine with him, and he with Me. Revelation 3:20 NKJV
6. For by grace you have been saved through faith, and that not of yourselves; *it is* the gift of God. Ephesians 2:8 NKJV
7. Who were born, not of blood, nor of the will of the flesh, nor of the will of man, but of God. John 1:13 NKJV
8. But has now been revealed by the appearing of our Savior Jesus Christ, *who* has abolished death and brought life and immortality to light through the gospel. 2 Timothy 1:10 NKJV
9. Strongs's Number G4806, Strong's concordance smart phone app.
10. But he who is joined to the Lord is one spirit *with Him.* 1 Corinthians 6:17 NKJV
11. But you *are* a chosen generation, a royal priesthood, a holy nation, His own special people, that you may proclaim the praises of Him who called you out of darkness into His marvelous light. 1 Peter 2:9 NKJV
12. Therefore lay aside all filthiness and overflow of wickedness, and receive with meekness the implanted word, which is able to save your souls. James 1:21 NKJV
13. For if anyone is a hearer of the word and not a doer, he is like a man observing his natural face in a mirror; for he observes himself, goes away, and immediately forgets what kind of man he was. James 1:23-24 NKJV

14. You are of God, little children, and have overcome them, because He who is in you is greater than he who is in the world. 1 John 4:4 NKJV

15. Whoever believes that Jesus is the Christ is born of God, and everyone who loves Him who begot also loves him who is begotten of Him. 1 John 5:1 NKJV

16. For as he thinks in his heart, so *is* he. Proverbs 23:7a NKJV

17. And I, brethren, could not speak to you as to spiritual *people* but as to carnal, as to babes in Christ. I fed you with milk and not with solid food; for until now you were not able *to receive it,* and even now you are still not able; for you are still carnal. For where *there are* envy, strife, and divisions among you, are you not carnal and behaving like *mere* men? 1 Corinthians 3:1-3 NKJV

18. God *is* faithful, by whom you were called into the fellowship of His Son, Jesus Christ our Lord. 1 Corinthians 1:9 NKJV

19. For the earnest expectation of the creation eagerly waits for the revealing of the sons of God. Romans 9:19 NKJV

20. Now to Abraham and his Seed were the promises made. He does not say, "And to seeds," as of many, but as of one, "And to your Seed," who is Christ. Galatians 3:16 NKJV

21. For all the promises of God in Him *are* Yes, and in Him Amen, to the glory of God through us. 2 Corinthians 1:20 NKJV

22. By which have been given to us exceedingly great and precious promises, that through these you may be partakers of the divine nature, having escaped the corruption *that is* in the world through lust. 2 Peter 1:4 NKJV

23. And if you *are* Christ's, then you are Abraham's seed, and heirs according to the promise. Galatians 3:29 NKJV

24. Therefore we also, since we are surrounded by so great a cloud of witnesses, let us lay aside every weight, and the sin which so easily ensnares *us,* and let us run with endurance the race that is set before us, looking unto Jesus, the author and finisher of *our* faith, who for the joy that was set before Him endured the cross, despising the shame, and has sat down at the right hand of the throne of God. Hebrews 12:1-2 NKJV

Chapter 5

HEALING THROUGH RIGHTEOUSNESS

That as **sin** hath reigned unto **death**, even so might **grace** reign through **righteousness unto eternal life** by Jesus Christ our Lord. Romans 5:21, KJV, emphasis mine

I have emphasised the keywords in the above scripture and it is important for us to understand the meaning of these words to learn to appropriate healing.

❖ What is Sin? There are many Greek words which are translated as *sin*. The most common meaning of sin is: *"to miss the mark for the prize."* So, when a born again believer misses the spirit and ends up in the flesh, he has sinned. It need not be an outright evil act, but even in subtle ways we can miss the spirit and land up in flesh.

For example, when Samuel went to the house of Jesse to anoint the next king of Israel, he looked at the muscular and tall sons of Jesse and thought to himself; surely this must be the next king! He was ready to anoint one of them, but God intervened and stopped him in his heart[1]. Samuel saw in the flesh and sinned (missed the mark). He repented immediately and corrected his course. This is the beauty of walking in the spirit. It doesn't mean that you will never sin (miss the mark). It means you will walk with a deep and satisfying awareness of God's voice in your heart. By creating an internal awareness of your righteousness, you will sharpen your inner ear to the spirit, so that as soon as you deviate from the spirit, you sense it and repent (change your mind) immediately.

The prize you enjoy is the fruit of the spirit (love, joy, peace, etc.) in your emotions and character. A sense of peace will be the core emotion of your life.

❖ What is death? Death is the manifestation of darkness or fruits of the flesh. This manifests as depression, despair, pain, bitterness, etc. Even sickness and disease is a form of death that robs the quality of life from us. Satan is the author of death[2] and by learning how to walk in the spirit we can escape his plan for us.

❖ What is Grace? It is the ability of God that is available to you because of His unmerited love and favour towards you. You have access to God's ability. By faith, only by faith, you access this ability [3].

❖ What is righteousness? Righteousness means *you are made as you should be in the spirit*. This is the essence of faith righteousness. By faith, you see yourself as righteous as Jesus Himself. You are clothed with the righteousness of Jesus which He obtained at the resurrection. This puts us in the league of victors and conquerors[4].

❖ What is *unto* eternal life? It means to bring *eternal life* into manifestation. Eternal life is the life God infused into your spirit at the new birth. It is the quality of life God possesses which can be known and experienced[5]. The best example of how eternal life looks like is seen in the life and ministry of Jesus. Jesus was unfazed over sickness, diseases, demons, and natural circumstances. He lived on top of poverty and needs. Over the top, abundant, and superfluous life! This is the life you and I possess in our spirit, and seldom have we accessed it. It's available inside us, and by faith, only by faith, we can actuate this life.

So, here is what the Apostle Paul is saying in the above Scripture.

When we miss the mark for the prize, we bring fruits of darkness into manifestation. However, when faith righteousness is established in our hearts; Grace (God's ability) flows seamlessly in and through our hearts and brings the life of God (which is in our spirit) into physical manifestation. This is the essence of the gospel message and this is the gospel the Apostle Paul preached.

Now, armed with this beautiful revelation, let's examine another scripture pertaining to healing and health.

And if Christ is in you, the body is dead because of sin, but the Spirit is life because of righteousness. But if the Spirit of Him who raised Jesus from the dead dwells in you, He who raised Christ from the dead will also give life to your mortal bodies through His Spirit who dwells in you. Romans 8:11-12 NKJV

I used to confess the above scripture relentlessly when my body was sick but never understood what it meant. Paul says that the body is dead because of sin. What could this mean? You see when you were born again it's your spirit that is made alive and healthy, but the body is the same. It's still part of the decay system initiated by Adam's sin.

IN ADAM WE WERE PROGRAMMED TO DIE.

In medical terms, this is called *apoptosis*, which means *programmed cell death*. When sin entered into mankind, our cells were programmed to die in Adam. Then Paul drops a bombshell of truth which I missed for many years. He goes on to say, the spirit is alive because of righteousness. Righteousness has been imparted into your spirit. Now, read the next line in this thought process; "The same Spirit who raised Jesus from the dead gives life to your mortal bodies." Our mortal bodies can experience resurrected life in this life!

If this is true, then all believers should be enjoying great health and never have sickness in their bodies, you may wonder! So, where is the disconnection?

What Paul is saying is this: Though our physical bodies are growing old and weak, exposed to the elements of the world, the Spirit of God can infuse resurrected life to it and give supernatural health to the body (until our mission on earth is finished). How? Because you have learnt to keep your heart in faith righteousness! This is the power of faith. You will understand this better on how to keep your heart in faith in the chapter on *Meditation-the key for healing and health.*

When you hold your heart in faith righteousness, then, only then you will experience the power of righteousness in your body and your behaviours. This is what it means, "With the heart, one believes unto righteousness.[6]"

Righteousness is the very nature of God. God's thoughts are righteous, His ways are righteous and His works are righteous. The gift of righteousness is restored in our recreated spirit[7]. The God whom we love and serve is a *God of faith*. Everything who God is and does is by faith. The gospel message the early Apostles preached revealed

RIGHTEOUSNESS EMPOWERS TO LIVE THE RESURRECTED LIFE.

the righteousness of God from faith to faith[8]. The faith to accept the gospel comes in the gospel. The gospel has the potential to take a sinner and make him stand right with God as if he or she has never sinned. Righteousness is not just merely a right standing before God alone, it's also a right standing before your adversaries which may be sickness, disease, poverty, pain etc. Many believers are oblivious to this aspect of righteousness. When you understand this aspect, your prayer life will leap to a new glorious level. You will take your authority in Christ and use it.

When describing the weapons of our spiritual warfare, the Apostle Paul refers to righteousness as the breastplate[9]. A breastplate is worn by a soldier to protect the heart. When one believes that Jesus was raised from the dead, the faith righteousness protects his heart from the corruption of sin. This is the primary way to guard your heart with all diligence[10]. When we guard our hearts with faith righteousness, all the issues of our lives will be resolved.

The benefits of believing that you are righteous by faith are many. It boosts one's faith, it gives freedom to fellowship with the Father, it restores son-ship, and it gives peace in your heart, and freedom from sin consciousness. Faith leaps from a heart that is established in faith righteousness. Now, you understand that faith is not as elusive as some have portrayed it to be in Christendom. Faith is just a natural response from a heart that is steadfast in believing that Jesus is our righteousness!

WHEN WE GUARD OUR HEARTS WITH FAITH RIGHTEOUSNESS, ALL THE ISSUES OF OUR LIVES WILL BE RESOLVED.

When you *believe* that you are *righteous by faith* it destroys Satan's work instantly in your life. To believe means to see with your heart. A believer is translated from the power of darkness into the kingdom of God[11]. Righteousness makes you as bold as a lion[12]. Righteousness by faith is the key that unlocks all the benefits that Christ offers in this life. This includes healing and health!

CIRCUMCISION CANNOT BE REVERSED

In my twenty years of medical practice, I have anaesthetised a large number of patients who came for surgical circumcision. Yet I have not seen one procedure where circumcision was reversed! Why? Because this is impossible to do, as the foreskin which is removed is destroyed and not stored for future re-attachment. Paul reveals that true circumcision is of the heart and not of the flesh (Romans 2:28). This is a marvellous revelation! At new birth, our old man, the sin nature, is immersed into the death of Christ (Romans 6:5, 6). If anyone is in Christ, he is a new creation! The old is gone, behold all things are made new (2 Corinthians 5:17). Can you see? Your old man, the foreskin of your heart is destroyed with the death of Christ and in its place, lives the resurrected Christ; the new man! [13]

Your old man no longer lives in an imaginary corner somewhere waiting to jump into you if you stumble in sin. Your righteousness is irreversible! I say it again YOUR RIGHTEOUSNESS IS IRREVERSIBLE. Your sins; past, present and future are forgiven and you are wiped clean! Your sins are not the issue standing between you and God; it's your un-renewed mind the issue. Ignorant of this truth, many believers are continuously in a 'confession mode' hoping that they will be worthy before Him.

SEALED WITH HIS SPIRIT

In Ephesians 1:13, Paul said, "In Him you also *trusted,* after you heard the word of truth, the gospel of your salvation; in whom also, having believed, you were sealed with the Holy Spirit of promise." Our union with Christ is sealed with the Holy Spirit of promise! This seal is not like a rubber stamp seal placed on us, but rather a sealing of a jar to preserve its contents. Your spirit is made new with the true righteousness and holiness and on top sealed with the Holy Spirit of promise never to be contaminated. If you are ignorant of this reality, you will not experience the joy and contentment of your new birth. Now, you are armed with this mighty revelation. You are already experiencing healing as this truth explodes inside you. This is the power of righteousness. David saw this coming in the New Covenant and longed to experience it.

Blessed are those, whose lawless deeds are forgiven, And whose sins are covered; Blessed is the man to whom the Lord shall not impute sin. Romans 4:7-8 NKJV

God cannot impute sin on a born again believer. This is a marvellous truth hidden from an average believer. It doesn't give us the license to sin; rather, it gives us boldness over the circumstances of life as no accusation can be levied against a believer by the evil one.

FAKE RIGHTEOUSNESS

If there is true righteousness, then there must be false righteousness too. This is the righteousness sold by religion, which constantly demands that you perform righteous deeds to become righteous. The Jewish Pharisees were obsessed with this kind of righteousness[14]. Don't fall into that trap! Guard your heart with the truth with all diligence! The laws and the commandments have been fulfilled on your behalf. Jesus wiped out the handwriting of requirements that was against us, which was contrary to us. And He has taken it out of the way, having nailed it to the cross. Having disarmed principalities and powers, He made a public spectacle of them, triumphing over them in it[15]. So, what is the purpose of the laws and commandments for a believer now?

The laws and the commandments no longer demand from a believer. It rather defines you now! You are in Christ, you have obtained righteousness. You are qualified to inherit all the promises that are promised in the Bible. Learn to look at the laws and the commandments with this new set of eyes. They are like pictures showing who you really are in Christ! After you have seen it in your heart, then act that way. This is why James exhorted his listeners to keep looking into the perfect law of liberty and act it out[16].

Some, in ignorance, are emotionally moved in meetings, go forward and make a commitment to do better next time and not to their surprise, they fail again. So they run from meetings to meetings, altar-calls to altar-calls, living in frustration. If you do this, you will confuse your heart. If you are one of those who constantly do such things, you need to take time and meditate and see your true image in Christ.

(If you sin, confess and repent before God. That's very healthy. But don't live with sin consciousness which made

109

you stumble in the first place! Confession is healthy, only if you do it from the place of faith. If you moved away from the place of faith, confession will work against you, as it will confuse your heart.)

Two Realities and Two Manifestations

When you believe that you are righteous in Christ, you are in faith and in God's reality. On the other hand, when you see yourself in the flesh, you are in the carnal reality. Which reality is going to dominate your life? It depends on which one you choose and make it as your heart belief. This is the core of walking in the spirit!

THE LAWS AND THE COMMANDMENTS DEFINE YOU NOW!

How to make information into a heart belief will be explained better further along.

Remember, both realities can exist at the same time while you are in the process of persuading your heart. As you stay focused on your spirit and see yourself living that reality in your heart, then, and only then, that reality will be established in your heart. With this in mind, you are ready to move on to the next chapter on *The Heart*.

Scripture Reference

1. So it was, when they came, that he looked at Eliab and said, "Surely the LORD's anointed *is* before Him!" But the LORD said to Samuel, "Do not look at his appearance or at his physical stature, because I have refused him. For *the* LORD *does* not *see* as man sees; for man looks at the outward appearance, but the LORD looks at the heart." 1 Samuel 16:6-7, NKJV

2. Inasmuch then as the children have partaken of flesh and blood, He Himself likewise shared in the same, that through death He might destroy him who had the power of death, that is, the devil. Hebrews 2:14 NKJV

3. Therefore, having been justified by faith, we have peace with God through our Lord Jesus Christ, through whom also we have access by faith into this grace in which we stand, and rejoice in hope of the glory of God. Romans 5:1-2, NKJV

4. Yet in all these things we are more than conquerors through Him who loved us. Romans 8:37, NKJV

5. And this is eternal life, that they may know You, the only true God, and Jesus Christ whom You have sent. John 17: 3, NKJV

6. For with the heart one believes unto righteousness, and with the mouth confession is made unto salvation. Romans 10:10, NKJV

7. For if by the one man's offense death reigned through the one, much more those who receive abundance of grace and of the gift of righteousness will reign in life through the One, Jesus Christ. Romans 5:17, NKJV

8. For in it the righteousness of God is revealed from faith to faith; as it is written, "The just shall live by faith." Romans 1:17, NKJV

9. Stand therefore, having girded your waist with truth, having put on the breastplate of righteousness. Ephesians 6:14, NKJV

10. Keep your heart with all diligence, For out of it *spring* the issues of life. Proverbs 4:23, NKJV

11. He has delivered us from the power of darkness and conveyed *us* into the kingdom of the Son of His love. Colossians 1:13, NKJV

12. The wicked flee when no one pursues, But the righteous are bold as a lion. Proverbs 28:1, NKJV

13. Therefore, if anyone *is* in Christ, *he is* a new creation; old things have passed away; behold, all things have become new. Now all things *are* of God, who has reconciled us to Himself through Jesus Christ, and has given us the ministry of reconciliation. 2 Corinthians 7:17-18, NKJV

14. What shall we say then? That Gentiles, who did not pursue righteousness, have attained to righteousness, even the righteousness of faith; but Israel, pursuing the law of righteousness, has not attained to the law of righteousness. Why? Because *they did* not *seek it* by faith, but as it were, by the works of the law. For they stumbled at that stumbling stone. Romans 9: 30-32, NKJV

15. Having wiped out the handwriting of requirements that was against us, which was contrary to us. And He has taken it out of the way, having nailed it to the cross. Colossians 2:14-15, NKJV

16. But he who looks into the perfect law of liberty and continues *in it,* and is not a forgetful hearer but a doer of the work, this one will be blessed in what he does. James 1:25 NKJV

SECTION B

Chapter 6

THE HEART

The word *heart* appears numerous times in both the Old and the New Testament, and there are subtle differences in what it means in different places in the Bible[1]. Understanding what it means in a particular passage helps us to grasp the practical application of that passage of scripture. Remember, our goal in studying any scripture is to see how it can be practically applied in day to day life! Therefore, a good working knowledge of the heart is vital. My presentation on this subject is a conceptual model. It's nearly impossible to accurately explain this to the satisfaction of a carnal mind. A conceptual understanding is sufficient for us to experience the truth for real-life transformation. Also, keep in mind that we are not looking at the anatomy of the human heart as in medical science; rather, we are trying to understand the *spiritual heart* and how it influences our physical body.

The heart is the real you, the seat of your believed identity[2]. I say believed identity because what you believe about your self is what will manifest in your life. As you start the journey of renewing your mind, you need to know the difference between true identity and believed identity clearly. Your true identity and your believed identity are different in the beginning, but as you renew your mind these two identities will begin to merge; you will understand this further along. The Apostle Paul said that even though the outer man is

THE HEART IS THE REAL YOU, THE SEAT OF YOUR BELIEVED IDENTITY.

perishing, yet the inner man is being renewed day by day[3]. This shows that there is a part of the heart which can be influenced and changed. This is not an automatic process, but one that happens as we renew our mind. The condition of your heart after you are born again is very different from the condition of your heart before you were born again[4]. Understanding this is very important! If you do not grasp this truth you will be confused at certain scriptures. Remember, in the Old Testament period, no one could be born again. This is because Christ had not yet come, died on the cross, and rose from the dead. However, the Old Testament saints were imputed with righteousness when they placed their trust in God who revealed Himself through types and shadows of Christ. Righteousness was credited to their account[5]. However, for us who live after the cross we are made righteous with Jesus.

In very simple terms, the heart is the combination of the spirit and the soul. Your inner man! The soul and the mind are one and the same. Emotions, will power and intellect are all function of the mind. Again, remember, this conceptual understanding is more than sufficient for the practical application of this truth.

The mind is made of the conscious mind (intellect) and subconscious mind (cellular memory). Memory is stored both in the conscious and in the subconscious mind. The conscious mind stores memories as information which can be recalled at will, whereas the subconscious mind stores information as deep feelings. When the subconscious mind is evoked, deep feelings begin to arise and they influence the conscious mind. Depending on what types of feelings are evoked, you will experience either emotion of joy or sadness in your conscious mind. Experiences of the past; either good or bad, are stored in the subconscious mind. That is why certain smells, certain pictures, certain words and even certain people can bring those feelings alive and you may feel joy or uneasiness depending on the original experience. When we came to Christ, we had a life time of information in our subconscious mind which was contrary to God's reality. This information was guiding the way we conducted our lives like an autopilot. Therefore, in our journey of following the Lord as a disciple, we are learning to rewrite the information in our subconscious mind with God's truth. Cutting edge medical science has shown that the subconscious mind is present in all the organs of the body. The organs of the whole body have the capacity to store cellular memories in them. David said in Psalm 51:6, "Behold, you desire truth in the inward parts, and in the hidden *part* you will make me to know wisdom." This is more a literal statement than a metaphor. With emerging scientific knowledge it looks like modern science is catching up with biblical wisdom.

Remember from the previous chapters, the spirit is dead or separated from God before the new birth. So, man is primarily functioning from a soulish realm. Spiritually dead men do not have the *light of life* inside them, and henceforth are darkened. Without light from the spirit, interpretation of the data received from the five senses is distorted in the intellectual mind. Since the time of Adam, men have created a world based on this distorted perception of the information (data) around them. Now you can understand why every good, man attempts, has so much chaos built into it. It looks like chaos is the new order! You can see this chaos in everything man has ever created. Religious, political, education, banking and health systems all have chaos in-built. They are constantly coming up with new ideas, which create more new problems. All these systems are born out of a mind which is operating independently of God. On the contrary, wisdom says, the blessing of the Lord makes one rich and He adds no sorrow to it.[6]

> **UNTIL WE CAME TO CHRIST, WE ALREADY HAVE CREATED A LIFETIME OF FAULTY PARADIGMS.**

In the book of Jeremiah, God declares,

The heart is deceitful above all things,

And desperately wicked;

Who can know it? Jeremiah 17:9, NKJV

(Remember, this is the condition of the heart of man before new birth)

The word *deceitful* in the above scripture can also be translated as 'showing footprints.' And the word *desperately wicked* can also be translated as 'incurably sick.' So, what God is saying is this: A heart that is showing footprints is incurably sick! [7]

Footprints are normally left after someone walks over. It looks like all the information we process in our conscious minds (by choice) has the potential to leaves a footprint in our subconscious mind (a part of the heart). When information elicits emotions in us, they leave an imprint in our subconscious minds. From childhood, our mind is developed by receiving information from outside. Then, we interpreted that information and passed judgements. Remember, we did not have the light inside us before the new birth. So, a mind functioning without light (from the spirit) interprets and analyses information in the darkness. As this is the only system of knowledge for growth available, we felt nothing abnormal about it. After all, everyone around us was also functioning in the same way. However, such faulty judgments and conclusions of data created a distorted paradigm. It is through this faulty paradigm we related to the outside world. This created further distortions and this

FEAR IS THE DOMINANT EMOTION OF THE FLESH

never-ending vicious cycle continued. Until we came to Christ (light), we already have created a lifetime of faulty paradigms. This faulty paradigm is the root cause of all the misery in all the areas of our lives. Our heart has been incurably sick!

Fear is the core emotion of spiritually dead men or in other words, fear is the dominant emotion of the flesh. We see this in Adam when he hid in the trees at the voice of God. Ever since man's perception about God changed because of sin, he is running away from God. Now, why was he afraid of God? After his spirit died (separated from God), man's interpretation of the voice of God was distorted; and this produced fear inside him. God's voice did not change but Adam's interpretation of that voice had changed! The paradigm of his world view in his heart had shifted! Nobody was threatening or chasing after Adam. Yet, he interpreted the voice of God as a threat, and he hid from God. Adam misunderstood his Father's voice and ever since God has been misunderstood! The truth about the God of love has been mangled in the dark hearts of man. Man lost the ability to understand the true nature of God. Now, man begins to blame God as the cause of all the problems, even though God is the only solution! He cannot see it because his heart is dark and has alienated himself from the life of God. The prodigal son left the house!

Spiritually dead men cannot understand the heart of God. Natural man cannot perceive the things of God as He is a spirit. Spiritually dead men cannot save themselves. Man's heart is incurably sick! He is spiritually blind, he cannot perceive the realm of the spirit, he is held captive to his own faulty paradigms which were created by distorted judgments, he has imprisoned himself to his own opinions. These are the hallmarks of a broken heart and with this, he has declared war on God!

Fear involves torment and perfect love is the only cure for fear. God is a loving Father and extends peace towards us. He wants to save us from this vicious spiral of darkness within our hearts which we have created. He wants to save us from ourselves! Without alleviating from the fear of judgment and condemnation, the heart cannot be healed. At the birth of Jesus, an angel appeared to a group of shepherds and announced a love letter from heaven, "Peace and goodwill towards man!"[8] Jesus is the light of the world who has come to set things right. Men who lived in darkness saw a marvellous light in Jesus[9]. Jesus is the answer this world desperately needs. He is the only answer, there is no other!

At the beginning of His ministry, Jesus turned to the book of Isaiah and read this portion of the scripture.

> The Spirit of the Lord is upon me, because he hath anointed me to preach the gospel to the poor; he hath sent me to heal the broken hearted, to preach deliverance to the captives, and recovering of sight to the blind, to set at liberty them that are bruised. Isaiah 61:1 NKJV

A broken heart is one that,

- ❖ Hath taken captive to its own imagination (creating faulty paradigms).
- ❖ Is blind to the realm of the spirit and can only perceive the natural realm.

❖ Is bruised and hardened (like a blood clot).

Now, can you see that without healing the heart any attempt to heal the physical body is vanity and grasping of the wind?

This is the condition of a man's heart before being born again. This is also the condition of a man who is born again but not walking after his born again spirit. As you understood from the previous discussions, at new birth God recreated our spirit. You will only experience, however, the benefits of the healed heart when you walk after the spirit. That is why Paul is exhorting all the believers to walk in the spirit, and not after the flesh.

The Apostle John was calling all believers to walk in the light and in the truth[10]. The terminologies are different but the message is the same; walk in the spirit/ truth/ light.

If a saved person is not walking in the spirit, he or she is deluded as much as the unsaved person. For the unsaved, the life of God is outside them, and they need this life desperately but by refusing it they have alienated themselves from it. For the saved, the life of God is inside them, in their spirit, but by not learning to walk after the spirit, they have alienated themselves from it, the end result? Both of them are walking in darkness. Both are sinning (missing the mark for the

WHEN YOU RECEIVED JESUS INTO THE HEART, THE SPIRIT OF CHRIST IS UNITED WITH THE SPIRIT PART OF YOUR HEART.

price), and missing on the benefits of God. When you received Jesus into the heart, the spirit of Christ is united with the spirit part of your heart. The heart is illuminated! You opened the door; the light came into your heart. Light, the word of God, the spirit of Christ, the life of God are all synonymous and interchangeably used throughout the scriptures. Through the spirit part of your heart, you are connected to God the Father! You are born again! The Apostle John calls those who are born again as those who are born from above! You have become citizens of heaven. This is best explained in the Amplified Bible as follows.

But to as many as did receive *and* welcome Him, He gave the right [the authority, the privilege] to become children of God, *that is*, to those who believe in (adhere to, trust in, and rely on) His name—who were born, not of blood [natural conception], nor of the will of the flesh [physical impulse], nor of the will of man [that of a natural father], but of God [that is, a divine and supernatural birth—they are born of God—spiritually transformed, renewed, sanctified]. John 1:12–13 AMP

However, your conscious mind and the subconscious mind are still the same. By new birth, you have started the journey; a journey of knowing God in your heart and writing the truth about your true identity in your subconscious mind. It's a lifelong journey whereby you are changed from glory to glory one situation at a time. Changing your mind is entirely in your hands and it's your responsibility. God has done His part, now he is inviting you to fulfil your part; renew the mind and enjoy the life of God!

Your life will transform only when you change the subconscious part of your heart. Only you have the power to influence the subconscious part of your heart. Neither God, nor the devil, nor any other human being has the power to influence the subconscious part of your heart. May be bad things have happened to you, but remember, it's your choice to attach significance to those things, and by this, you have allowed it to influence your heart. The good news is you can change your heart again by choice. David said in Psalm 19:7, "The law of the Lord is perfect converting the soul." The word of God has the potential to redesign your life no matter how bad it has been scarred by the past negative experiences. As the subconscious part of your heart changes, you will experience transformation.

Now let's see how to positively influence and change the subconscious part of your heart. Please consider the following exhortation to believers by the Apostle Paul.

This I say, therefore, and testify in the Lord, that you should no longer walk as the rest of the Gentiles walk, in the futility of their mind, having their understanding darkened, **being alienated from the life of God, because of the ignorance**, because of the blindness of their heart; who, being past feeling, have given themselves over to lewdness, to work all uncleanness with greediness.

But you have not so learned Christ, if indeed you have heard Him and have been taught by Him, as the truth is in Jesus. Ephesians 4:17-21, NKJV, emphasis mine

124

The above picture is of one who has alienated himself from the life of God. *The keyword is ignorance.* But to believers, he says, you have not so learned Christ. Learning Christ means to have gained accurate information about what Christ has accomplished for us.

The renewing of your subconscious mind starts with accurate knowledge of what Christ has done through the death, burial and the resurrection. This is the starting point of transformation. Accurate knowledge is important to renew the mind. This is best illustrated in the following scripture,

That the **sharing** of your faith may become effective by the **acknowledgment** of every good thing which is in you in Christ Jesus. Philemon 1:6, NKJV emphasis mine

The word acknowledgement in the above scripture is translated from the Greek word *epignosis*, which means *accurate knowledge*. The Apostle Paul wants believers everywhere to gain *accurate knowledge* of who God is and what He has done for us in the death, burial and the resurrection of Jesus Christ. Without accurate knowledge, you will not desire to participate in the renewing of your mind which is the only way to transformation. I cannot overemphasize this enough! This is the reason why

WITHOUT ACCURATE KNOWLEDGE YOU WILL NOT DESIRE TO PARTICIPATE IN THE RENEWING OF YOUR MIND.

the Apostles took time to write the epistles to the churches.

The word *sharing* in the above verse is translated from the Greek word *koinonia*, which means a partnership or joint participation. If you do not have accurate information, you will not participate in the fellowship with Jesus (who lives in your spirit). As you keep acknowledging your position, the faith to live the shared life flows seamlessly. Again, this is not mere mental information that we are seeking, but through accurate information, we are aiming to experience the truth in the heart. This happens during meditation as we shall see in the next chapter.

The heart is the real you. How you perceive yourself in your heart is the way you behave in life. This is what it means *as a man thinketh in his heart so is he in Proverbs 23:7*. This is talking about the deep thoughts from the subconscious part of the heart. So, when you change your image in the subconscious part of your mind, your external realities change effortlessly. People with broken heart do not have a healthy sense of self. Therefore, they are seeking acceptance and approval from others all the time. In this state they are either seeking control or allowing others to control them. However, when they renew their mind, they settle in their identity and have peace within themselves. This internal sense of peace creates harmony within them and confidence towards man and God. They are no longer seeking external approval, they are experiencing their completeness in Christ.

Wisdom is crying out to guard our hearts with all diligence because for out of the heart springs the issues of life[11]. As you influence your heart with God's word, the issues of life will be resolved. If sickness is an issue in your life, it can be resolved with God's word. The whole purpose of this book is to get you to understand this! If you did not understand this, you will never move into victory. Even if you did, you will not sustain it. Only after we understand this we will take responsibility. Instead of blaming everything and everyone, we will humble ourselves and go to God's word and do what Jesus told us to do i.e. to apply His word in our hearts.

In summary,

- ❖ The heart is the combination of spirit, conscious mind & subconscious mind.
- ❖ At new birth, your spirit is renewed and recreated, the word of God lives in the spirit part of you.
- ❖ Accurate information is a must for the conscious mind to engage.
- ❖ The subconscious mind can only be influenced through the meditation process.

As the whole heart becomes healthy, you experience transformation. The healed heart (wholesome heart) changes your world view. In this new paradigm, you will begin to operate in peace and tranquillity. This is what it means in Proverbs 14:30, "A sound heart is life to the body!" It's not a metaphor, it's a literal statement! The ability to find good in life depends on the condition of your heart. A crooked or perverse heart will find no good (Proverbs 17:20). If born again believers do not function with their minds focused on their spirit, they will create distortions in their hearts. Only a wholesome heart is life to the body, a crooked heart is the source of all the misery. Ignorant of this we often blame the devil for all the pain, but what is much needed is to get the heart healed. Remember, there is a devil that is walking about seeking whom he may devour. However, the devil has an inroad only when we walk in the flesh. Paul said we should not give room to the devil (Ephesians 4:27). Meaning, when we walk in the flesh we give room to the devil. Walking in the spirit entails a conscious and deep awareness of who you are in Christ. When this is your dominant thinking, you function in peace and thanksgiving as your default mode of operation.

SUBCONSCIOUS MIND

The subconscious mind cannot be accurately located in the body. The subconscious mind is more like an autopilot. It governs everything about you without you knowing consciously. Medical research in neuropsychiatry reveals that the subconscious mind is present in the cells of every organ. They call it as cellular memories. The whole subject on the mind is an enigma even to the most modern cognitive neuroscientist. In my view, in the area of mind, medical science is catching up with biblical wisdom.

In the book of Proverbs we read exhortations like: *write the truth in your heart, bind them continually on your heart, keep them in the midst of your heart* etc. As you study the word and gain accurate knowledge about the cross, the love of God, new birth, etc., and

THE SUBCONSCIOUS MIND GOVERNS EVERYTHING ABOUT YOU.

spend time on meditation, you will start writing the information in your subconscious mind. This is what it means to write the truth in your heart[12]. Remember, this information is already in your spirit. As you meditate, you are transforming the reality of your spirit into your subconscious mind through the conscious mind. Information plus emotion leads to writing the truth in the heart. Unless you see the information in a way that affects your identity, that information will not be written in your subconscious mind.

The written word of God was given to educate our conscious mind, which is the beginning of the transformation process. However, it only comes alive in your heart during active meditation as we shall see in the next chapter. You will recall from the chapter on the new birth, how the word of God is implanted in your spirit. The Apostle James encourages believers to receive the implanted word with meekness[13]. What does it mean *to receive* the implanted word? James is asking believers to continuously look at the law of liberty with an intention to do God's word. You *receive* in your conscious mind what has already been implanted in your spirit. The word "do" is translated from a Greek word which means *poetic performer*. A poet is someone who is using all his emotions, words, and body gestures to express information. This is a form of meditation! Your born again spirit is not accessible to the five senses. If the five senses are not engaged, the conscious mind cannot grasp. So, God gave us the written word for us to renew our mind. As you keep looking at God's word and meditate on it (poetically perform), you transfer the reality to your subconscious mind.

Information plus emotion leads to writing the truth in the heart (subconscious mind). Then your whole body will be full of light. The key to transformation is meditation and by which you are wrapping yourself around the truth.

Jesus said;

> "No one, when he has lit a lamp, puts it in a secret place or under a basket, but on a lampstand, that those who come in may see the light. The lamp of the body is the eye. Therefore, when your eye is good, your whole body also is full of light. But when your eye is bad, your body also is full of darkness. Therefore, take heed that the light which is in you is not darkness. If then your whole body is full of light, having no part dark, the whole body will be full of light, as when the bright shining of a lamp gives you light." Luke 11:33-36 NKJV

"Eyes" in the above scripture means *focus*. In the Hebrew language knowledge is compared to light and ignorance is compared to darkness. As you focus your conscious mind in the word, the light that is already in your spirit begins to move from the spirit part of you to the subconscious mind. When this happens, you have put the lamp on the lampstand, so to speak. Now your whole body will be full of light with no part dark. Sickness (a form of darkness) simply falls off your body. No matter what the nature of your condition; be it genetic/inherited or environmentally acquired, darkness has to leave because the light has come. You will not only get healed but begin to enjoy health. You would have moved into a life of supernatural experiences. This is just the beginning of experiencing eternal life! Remember, Jesus is giving us incredible wisdom and it's our responsibility to engage in the process. Renewing your mind is not an option, but mandatory to experience resurrection power. If we don't engage in the process, then we have put the light under the basket, by doing so we have covered the light with darkness. In another place Jesus said, "If the light that is in you is darkness, how great that darkness will be!"[15]

Scripture Reference & Endnotes

1. In Matthew 15:19, Jesus says, out of the heart comes all sorts of wickedness. Here, the heart refers to the conscious and subconscious mind of a person who is not born again or a person who is born again but not led by the spirit.
   In 1.Peter 3:4, Peter talks about the hidden part of the heart which is the spirit.
   In the parable of the sower in Mark 4, Jesus said as soon as the seed fell in the heart, Satan came and grabbed the seed away. Here, the heart refers to the conscious mind. This person did not take time to meditate. His thinking is so set on worldly ways; the message from the preacher is not even registering in his mind.
2. For as he thinks in his heart, so *is* he. "Eat and drink!" he says to you, But his heart is not with you. Proverbs 23:7, NKJV
3. As in water face *reflects* face, So a man's heart *reveals* the man. Proverbs 27:19, NKJV, emphasis mine
4. Therefore we do not lose heart. Even though our outward man is perishing, yet the inward *man* is being renewed day by day. 2 Corinthians 4:16, NKJV
5. Therefore, if anyone *is* in Christ, *he is* a new creation; old things have passed away; behold, all things have become new. And therefore "it was accounted to him for righteousness." Romans 4:22, NKJV
6. The blessing of the LORD makes *one* rich, And He adds no sorrow with it. Proverbs 10:22, NKJV
7. Theological Wordbook of the Old Testament. Word no: 1676c, showing footprints. Word no: 135, incurably sick.
8. Glory to God in the highest, And on earth peace, goodwill toward men! Luke 2:14, NKJV
9. The people who sat in darkness have seen a great light,
10. And upon those who sat in the region and shadow of death Light has dawned. Matthew 4:16, NKJV
11. But if we walk in the light as He is in the light, we have fellowship with one another, and the blood of Jesus Christ His Son cleanses us from all sin. 1 John 1:7, NKJV
12. Keep your heart with all diligence, For out of it *spring* the issues of life. Proverbs 4:23, NKJV

13. Bind them on your fingers; Write them on the tablet of your heart. Proverbs 7:3, NKJV

14. Therefore lay aside all filthiness and overflow of wickedness, and receive with meekness the implanted word, which is able to save your souls. James 1:21, NKJV

15. But if your eye is bad, your whole body will be full of darkness. If therefore the light that is in you is darkness, how great is that darkness! Matthew 6:23 NKJV

Chapter 7

MEDITATION- THE KEY TO HEALING & HEALTH

Meditation in your heart is the missing link between having the resurrection power of God in your spirit and experiencing it in your daily life. Meditation has been the lifestyle of the renowned men and women of the Bible and the Bible is full of such exhortations. But what is meditation? Meditation is the process whereby you see/picture the reality of God's word in your heart and keep seeing it until that's the only reality in your heart. It also means to roll it over in your imagination. When you see how your life will look like if that particular truth is real in your life now, then you are doing biblical meditation. Merely thinking about the verse in the intellectual mind is not meditation.

Before we go into the details, I want to show two examples, one from the Old Testament and one from the New Testament as to what meditation of God's word does to your physical body.

Example 1

Caleb was a man who went to conquer the Anakim giants at the age of 85. His conversation with Joshua recorded in the book of Joshua chapter 14 reveals a very important wisdom key for divine health[1]. Moses sent 12 spies to spy the land of Canaan. Caleb was 40 years old when he was picked up to go with them. Caleb and Joshua brought back a good report while others brought back an evil report[2]. Because of the evil report, the children of Israel could not enter the Promised Land immediately. They had to wait for another 45 years. Caleb, now 85 years old, narrates to Joshua what he reported to Moses as it was **in his heart**, while others reported how they saw it with their eyes. Caleb saw the same situation, but his assessment was based on what God had already spoken to the children of Israel. He took the spoken word of God into his heart, and his paradigm changed. From that paradigm, he saw them well able to conquer the giants in the land. But because of the unbelief of the others, the Israelites could not enter into the Promised Land. Even though he was 85, he had the strength of a 40–year–old person. How? Because, his heart had arrested his strength based on the reality he had created in his heart. Right here is the secret of healthy living! God's spoken word was in his heart and his confession of the mouth was in line with his heart. Faith comes alive when God's word, the picture in your heart and the confession of the mouth synchronizes. This is how faith works. This is the wisdom of God available to everyone. Healthy living is how you see yourself in your heart based on His word.

Example 2

The Apostle Paul suffered a shipwreck and landed at the island of Malta[3]. On the shore, while gathering sticks to light a fire, a venomous snake bites him. To the surprise of the natives of the island, the poison did not have any effect on Paul's body. How can this be? The snake was real, the bite was real and the poison was spreading in the body of Paul, yet something stronger neutralized the power of the venom.

What Jesus had spoken about those who believe in His name had come true in Paul's situation. Jesus said if you drink anything deadly, it will not harm you. Jesus is talking about

IN MEDITATION WE CREATE PICTURES IN OUR HEART.

a breed of people who are masters of the circumstances, like Himself[4]. These are not superstitious beliefs. This is the reality of the life of faith. Sadly, we never gave thought to these words of the master. The wisdom of God has been lost in the translation! Paul was a man of faith. His reality was based on the words of Jesus and His doctrine. Paul's life was a life of meditation on God's word and the reality in his heart was based on the resurrection power. The Spirit had given life to the mortal body of Paul[5].

Many have equated meditation to memorization. People have memorized a lot of scriptures but it has not worked for them. Sadly, they have not done what the Bible exhorts to do. Meditate!

In meditation, we create pictures in our heart based on the promises of God. For example, if you are unable to walk, then based on the truth *by his stripes you are healed*; you see yourself get up, walk, run and do everything which your physical body does not permit you to do. You keep seeing this long enough until this is the only reality or picture you see in your heart. When your heart is fully persuaded, faith leaps out and at some point, you will start walking pain-free. When you ponder on truth and create emotions in your soul, you are writing that truth in your heart. Unless you see a truth from the perspective of how it will change your identity, it will not become a belief of your heart.

YOUR FAITH WILL ONLY WORK WITHIN THE BOUNDARIES OF YOUR HEART BELIEF.

Your faith will only work within the boundaries of your heart belief. Since the heart is the real you, what your heart believes is what you will experience in your life. This is the miracle of the heart! This is the way every man of God functioned in the Bible, yet such knowledge is lost for the 21st-century intellectual minds. Yet, if you are willing to surrender your opinion and follow His instructions, it will work perfectly for you.

Phrases like waiting on God, abiding in Him, dwelling in His presence, dwelling in the secret place, entering into the secret place, are all different ways of expressing the same thing- meditation!

WAITING ON GOD

The Hebrew meaning of the word *to wait* means to intertwine or to twist upon. Remember, God is already present in your spirit through His Spirit. Now, you are redirecting the focus of your mind and wrapping it around your spirit (which is the spirit of Christ/word of God/Holy Spirit). When this happens, you are meditating or waiting on God. You keep seeing in your heart what your life would be like if those promises are real in your life now. You are creating a new reality contrary to the reality of the five senses.

The book of Song of Solomon is a story of a loving relationship between a king and his lover and has phrases like these; *the king has come to the table (Song of Solomon 1:12), the king has brought me into his chamber (Song of Solomon 1:4).* All these are word pictures of our union with Christ in our spirit. All it needs is for us to keep our mind focused on who we are in the spirit. This is what it means to be spiritually minded. Nothing more and nothing less! In Isaiah 41:31, we read that those who wait on the Lord shall renew their strength and will rise above like an eagle with renewed strength. Waiting on God transforms our life; spirit, soul and body!

THE VINE IS THE CHRIST IN US AND WE ARE THE BRANCHES

ABIDING IN THE VINE

In John chapter 15, Jesus gave us another picture about meditation: Abiding in the vine!

> I am the vine; you are the branches. If you remain in me and I in you, you will bear much fruit; apart from me you can do nothing. If you do not remain in me, you are like a branch that is thrown away and withers; such branches are picked up, thrown into the fire and burned. If you remain in me and my words remain in you, ask whatever you wish, and it will be done for you.
> John 15:5–7 NIV

The vine is Jesus and we are the branches. To be more precise, the vine is our spirit in which Jesus lives by His word and our minds are the branches. When we stay our mind on the spirit (spiritually minded), then we are abiding in the vine, so to speak. Staying our mind on Jesus means to constantly remind ourselves of our oneness with Him and all the good things (health, healing, provision, vision, direction etc.) that we have in Him. Jesus was giving us the secret of bearing fruits in our lives. When we don't acknowledge the good things that are in us (in Christ that is), we wither away. Therefore, the options are either bearing fruits or withering away. There is no in-between or third option!

About abiding in the vine in another place, Jesus said, "He who eats my body and drinks my blood is he who abides in me[6]." Physiologically, after we eat food the blood supply to the intestines increases. This is to aid with digestion and to mobilize the nutrients that are digested. The absorbed nutrients are carried away by the blood to the cells for making proteins causing the growth of the natural body. Eventually the food that is absorbed becomes part of the body. Likewise, when we create realities in our imagination (heart) based on the absolute truth of God's promises, the Holy Spirit who is our lifeblood, zooms into our heart, and carries that reality into every cell of the body giving supernatural strength and energy. This becomes our believed identity! This is what it means *the Spirit gives life to the mortal body!* (Romans 8:11)

What I am writing here is profound biblical wisdom. But it is foolishness to the carnal mind. We can surrender our opinion and take His wisdom or hold on to our carnal opinion and lose the benefit of eternal life in our spirit. It's our choice and it's our responsibility!

PERFECT PEACE

You will keep him in perfect peace,

Whose mind is stayed on You,

Because he trusts in You. Isaiah 26:3, NKJV

The word *mind* in the above scripture is translated from a Hebrew word which should be more accurately translated as *imagination.* To imagine means to conceive in your mind and to give shape in your thoughts. We all know how to do this negatively, but have never trained ourselves to use God's word and construct a positive picture about ourselves. You see perfect peace is not something God withholds from you and will give it to you when you spend hours begging Him. Perfect peace is the by-product of keeping one's mind on His Word. There is power in positive imagination. You cannot function in hope without a positive imagination. Hope means confidant expectation of good things to come and this expectation is based on your capacity to imagine.

The promises of God are not for us just to memorize. It is for us to take them and create a picture of our lives in our imagination. When we do that in our hearts, faith leaps and brings that reality into manifestation. This is the ONLY way faith works. This is somehow hidden from most of us in the church. Imagination is a God given capacity for us to function and shape our world.

In the book of Joshua we read an interesting event about Joshua commanding the sun to stand still in the midst of the battle (Joshua 10). Until that point in history, there was no recorded incidence of anybody speaking to the planets in the Bible. How did such a novice idea enter into the heart of Joshua in the midst of a fight? You see, when Joshua took over from Moses as the leader of Israel, God told him to meditate on the Laws and the Commandments day and night and not to let it depart from his lips, to have good success (Joshua 1:8).

WHEN YOU WALK IN RESURRECTION POWER, YOUR LIFE WILL MIRROR THE LIFE OF JESUS.

When one does that, it changes the way how you perceive yourself in relation to your circumstances. Biblical faith has no bounds and you become a mountain mover! Teaching about changing your perspective, this is what Jesus meant when he said, "he who understands the word, produced a greater harvest from his heart." His word in your heart is the victory that overcomes every obstacle. The word "understanding" in the Greek could also mean deep thoughts of the heart. Deep thinking are nothing but focused imagination!

FELLOWSHIPPING WITH HIM

God is faithful, by whom you were called into the fellowship of His Son, Jesus Christ our Lord. 1 Corinthians 1:9

The word *fellowship* is translated from the Greek word *koinonia*. This word means partnership/intercourse/joint participation. This is an active process in which there is an exchange between two people in a very intimate way. Two becoming one! When we focus our minds on the death, burial and resurrection of Jesus, we are actively participating in the cross. This is where his death becomes our death and his resurrection becomes our resurrection. The Apostle Paul explains how he did this in the following passage,

And be found in Him, not having my own righteousness, which is from the law, but that which is through faith in Christ, the righteousness which is from God by faith; that I may know Him and the power of His resurrection, and the fellowship of His sufferings, being conformed to His death, if, by any means, I may attain to the resurrection from the dead. Philippians 3: 9-11 NKJV

Paul wanted to experience resurrection power in his life and ministry. First and foremost he established himself in faith righteousness. And then, to experience the resurrection life, he is wrapping his mind around the sufferings of Jesus on the cross. He is seeing himself die on the cross and be buried with Him. The word *"attain to"* in the above scripture means to *arrive at*. So, Paul is creating a reality in his heart through meditation on the cross that he may arrive at the resurrection, and experience the resurrection power in his life and ministry. When you walk in resurrection power, your life will mirror the life of Jesus. God wants us to walk in resurrection power in every area of our lives.

For the same reason, Paul said, "We proclaim the Lord's death" when we take communion[7]. By proclaiming His death, we are seeing the death of our old man in Him. To see the death of our old man is the starting point in this fellowship process. Even taking communion is a form of meditation whereby we are influencing our hearts with God's reality. I have explained this more in the next chapter on The Lord's Table.

SCIENCE AND MEDITATION

Research has proven that as you go into a deeper state of meditation, the brain waves go into slower wave pattern called the *alpha waves*. When you are awake and alert, the brain waves are predominantly *beta waves*. But as soon as you close your eyes, the brain waves switch to *alpha waves*. Then, as you calm down further with the mind focused or by adding music while keeping your eyes closed, deeper levels of alpha waves are reached. In this state you are in touch with the spirit part of the heart. It is in this state, the beliefs of your heart are easily changed. In this state, when you start picturizing yourself living the promises of God, they get imprinted in your heart and your life paradigm changes.

The *alpha wave* state of the brain is easily attained in the early mornings. This is the reason people hear God's voice better early in the morning more than other times of the day. It's not that God shows up early in the morning, but that we are more attuned to His voice early in the morning because we are more aware of the voice of our heart. God is present with us 24/7, His presence doesn't fluctuate! Even dancing, lifting hands, and swaying the body, have all been shown to calm the brain into alpha waves. This is the reason, praise and worship can be an incredible way to connect with God in your heart.

By learning to commune with God in our heart, we are connecting with Him. We are creating awareness so real; *Christ in you* becomes the dominant thought of our lives for every situation we face. Meditation is the key process whereby we enter into His presence and learn to live there.

Scripture Reference

1. I *was* forty years old when Moses the servant of the LORD sent me from Kadesh Barnea to spy out the land, and I brought back word to him as *it was* in my heart. Nevertheless my brethren who went up with me made the heart of the people melt, but I wholly followed the LORD my God. So Moses swore on that day, saying, 'Surely the land where your foot has trodden shall be your inheritance and your children's forever, because you have wholly followed the LORD my God.' And now, behold, the LORD has kept me alive, as He said, these forty-five years, ever since the LORD spoke this word to Moses while Israel wandered in the wilderness; and now, here I am this day, eighty-five years old. As yet I *am as* strong this day as on the day that Moses sent me; just as my strength *was* then, so now *is* my strength for war, both for going out and for coming in. Now therefore, give me this mountain of which the LORD spoke in that day; for you heard in that day how the Anakim *were* there, and *that* the cities *were* great *and* fortified. It may be that the LORD *will be* with me, and I shall be able to drive them out as the LORD said." Joshua 14:7-12 NKJV

2. Then Caleb quieted the people before Moses, and said, "Let us go up at once and take possession, for we are well able to overcome it." Numbers 13: 30 NKJV

3. But when Paul had gathered a bundle of sticks and laid *them* on the fire, a viper came out because of the heat, and fastened on his hand. So when the natives saw the creature hanging from his hand, they said to one another, "No doubt this man is a murderer, whom, though he has escaped the sea, yet justice does not allow to live." But he shook off the creature into the fire and suffered no harm. However, they were expecting that he would swell up or suddenly fall down dead. But after they had looked for a long time and saw no harm come to him, they changed their minds and said that he was a god. Acts 28:3-6 NKJV

4. And these signs will follow those who believe: In My name they will cast out demons; they will speak with new tongues; they will take up serpents; and if they drink anything deadly, it will by no means hurt them; they will lay hands on the sick, and they will recover." Mark 16:17-18 NKJV

5. But if the Spirit of Him who raised Jesus from the dead dwells in you, He who raised Christ from the dead will also give life to your mortal bodies through His Spirit who dwells in you. Romans 8:11 NKJV

6. For My flesh is food indeed, and My blood is drink indeed. He who eats My flesh and drinks My blood abides in Me, and I in him. John 6:55-56 NKJV

7. For as often as you eat this bread and drink this cup, you proclaim the Lord's death till He comes. 1 Corinthians 11:26 NKJV

Chapter 8

THE LORD'S TABLE

On the night he was betrayed, Jesus initiated the breaking of the bread and the wine which we call it the communion of the Lord's Table. It is very important that we understand why Jesus wanted His disciples to do this often. Since we are His disciples too, we should do this as often as we can. The power of remembering the death of the Lord Jesus is very often underestimated.

Jesus asked His disciples to do this often in remembrance of Him. Why has the Lord asked us to remember Him this way? What could be the reason? Could it be that when we participate in communion with all of our capacity that it will influence our hearts? Let's examine that!

For I received from the Lord that which I also delivered to you: that the Lord Jesus on the same night in which He was betrayed took bread; and when He had given thanks, He broke it and said, "Take, eat; this is My body which is]broken for you; do this in remembrance of Me." In the same manner He also took the cup after supper, saying, "This cup is the new covenant in My blood. This do, as often as you drink it, in remembrance of Me." For as often as you eat this bread and drink this cup, you proclaim the Lord's death till He comes. 1 Corinthian 11:23-26 NKJV emphasis mine.

In the above passage of scripture, the Apostle Paul throws some light on what this remembrance entails. Paul received revelation knowledge from the Lord about partaking in communion and how it will bless the church in the area of healing and health. By partaking in communion, the Apostle Paul said we are proclaiming the Lord's death until He comes. Why should we proclaim the Lord's death? Let us examine this a bit closer.

IN JESUS THE FLESH LOST ITS POWER.

HIS CROSS IS YOUR CROSS

On the cross, the Lord Jesus cried out with a loud voice and gave up His spirit[1]. He died on the cross and His lifeless body was hanging on the cross till it was buried. When sin was placed on Him, He died in the spirit first. Then he died on the natural. When Adam sinned in the beginning, **the flesh was born.** The flesh is the most powerful force in this world. It has the power to oppose God. Satan has no power as such; he is using man's power, which is the flesh. When Jesus the last Adam[2] became sin and died on the cross for us, **the flesh died!** On the cross, the power of the flesh was broken. A soldier took a spear and pierced the chest and ruptured the heart of Jesus, blood and water gushed out[3]. The blood that gives life to the body was shed. So the body of Jesus that was buried in the tomb had every other organ except blood. From the book of Leviticus[4], we know that the life of the flesh is in the blood. Here we see that the blood that gives life to the flesh of Jesus was poured out. Therefore, in Jesus, the flesh lost its power. Satan is the root of all evil but the only way he overpowers us is through the flesh. When we are in the flesh, he will find an inroad to attack us. The good news is that we are in the spirit[5] and by yielding to the spirit, we can walk a supernatural life. Satan will have no hold on us.

The Apostle Paul said, "Those who are in Christ' have crucified their flesh with its desire and its passions.[6]" The death of Jesus on the cross is my death. By proclaiming His death, I am actually proclaiming the death of my flesh with all its passions and desires. So when flesh tries to raise its head, I simply direct my focus to the cross. This is what it means *to take up your cross*. On the cross Jesus became you. The cross He carried was your cross. Now, he wants you to remember in communion His death as your death and thereby take up your cross. His cross is your cross!

PARTICIPATING IN THE EXCHANGE

When participating in communion we are using all our capacity to see His death as our death. The death of the flesh! Our flesh died! The blood that gives life to the flesh is poured out. The blood pouring out of His body is a graphic picture of the complete death of the flesh. Therefore when you take communion you are remembering and proclaiming the death of your own flesh. This is the key to victory! To experience resurrection life, to see yourself raised together with Him, first and foremost you have to see your death on the cross. This is what communion does to you. The word communion means joint participation. You are jointly participating in His death. You are seeing the death of Jesus on the cross as the death of your flesh. It becomes real in your heart. This is what it means when Paul said you are planted together in the likeness of his death in Romans chapter six[7.] What I am sharing here is very powerful. You should take time to contemplate this and see it in your heart and make it your revelation.

So now there is no condemnation for those who belong to Christ Jesus. And because you belong to him, the power of the life-giving Spirit has freed you from the power of sin that leads to death. Romans 8:1-2 NLT

Before you were born again, you were in the flesh. You were under the law of sin and death. That was the only reality for you. But now after you are born again, you are in the spirit. You have been ushered into the law of the spirit of life. Now, you can choose to make that your reality in your heart. And communion helps a great deal to influence your heart with this truth.

Grace made it possible for us to enter the realm of the spirit. Now, God is waiting for you to grasp this truth and enter into fellowship with Him in the realm of the spirit. This is what it means to be seated together with Him in the heavenly places[8]. The phrase *Heavenly places* means the spirit realm.

WHEN YOU ARE IN THE SPIRIT, YOU ARE UNDER THE LAW OF THE SPIRIT OF LIFE.

By taking part in communion you are saying, I am no longer in the flesh, I am in the spirit. The flesh has no power over me. I see my death in His death. Satan is the author of all sickness and disease. However, Satan can only bring sickness and disease in your body through the power of the flesh. When you are in the flesh and walk in the flesh, you give room for darkness to invade your life. The work of darkness includes sickness and disease. The good news is, you can break the power of darkness as you partake in communion, and boldly proclaim His death. Sickness simply leaves your body.

WORTHY OR UNWORTHY

Therefore whoever eats this bread or drinks this cup of the Lord in an unworthy manner will be guilty of the body and blood of the Lord. But let a man examine himself, and so let him eat of the bread and drink of the cup. For he who eats and drinks in an unworthy

153

manner eats and drinks judgment to himself, not discerning the Lord's body. 1 Corinthians 11:27-29 NKJV

Religious minds have completely mangled the above scripture and brought condemnation in the hearts of believers for centuries. All this is because we did not understand the finished work of Jesus on the cross. Instead of being encouraged to see their death on the cross, a believer is encouraged to take an inventory of their flesh when taking communion. Remember flesh stinks! If you approach the communion table with the mindset of what is wrong with me, you empower the flesh. You are now carnally minded. But on the other hand, if you participate in remembering what has been made right about you, you will be in the spirit and you are spiritually-minded. Remember in Christ you are made worthy!

(If you have sinned by yielding to the flesh, repent, confess and bounce back to the spirit quickly. Don't linger in your flesh for long. The key to deliverance from any habitual sins is not to see yourself unworthy, but rather to proclaim by faith your worth in Christ.)

What makes you worthy before God is not how clean your flesh is, rather your union with Christ. Only when you see yourself united with Christ you are judging your-self correctly. You have judged that your flesh is dead in His flesh. Now that your life is hidden in Him, you are worthy to take part in communion. You are complete in Him! If you are not taking communion from this perspective and taking stock of your flesh, you are taking communion in an unworthy manner. You will pass on a wrong judgment about yourself and end up in condemnation. Condemnation empowers your flesh! Satan's main weapon is condemnation. If he can get you to see yourself condemned, he will then rule over you! Condemnation is at the root of all sickness and diseases.

Remember what Jesus said; "He who eats His body and drinks His blood, it is he who abides in Him[9]." As you participate in communion, remember His death, and see yourself dead in Him. As you partake in this way, the Holy Spirit zooms into your heart and pumps the life of Christ into every cell of your body. If the church takes

CONDEMNATION EMPOWERS THE FLESH.

communion with this knowledge, there cannot be any sick or feeble among us. I envision a day when the church of Jesus Christ will grasp this truth and walk like a divine superman and superwoman on this earth before the second coming of the Lord. This may sound foolish, but the wisdom of God is foolishness to our carnal mind. But it is the power of God if one chooses to believe (see) in his or her heart and act on it.

JUDGING YOURSELF CORRECTLY

For he who eats and drinks in an unworthy manner eats and drinks judgement to himself, not discerning the Lord's body. For this reason, **many are weak and sick among you**, and many sleep. 1 Corinthians 11:29-30 NKJV emphasis mine

As a medical doctor when I read this statement; "For this reason, many are weak and sick" I jumped in excitement.

These are definitive terms and such life-giving reassuring words cannot be found in the medical world. While the whole medical world is spending an enormous amount of money to find a cure for many diseases, the wisdom of God comes along in very simple lines. Here Paul is not saying this may be one of the reasons for our sickness, rather he is saying it in definitive terms; FOR THIS REASON!

You see every sickness and disease went into His body when He was made sin on the cross. Now, you should see your sickness go into His body with all the capacity you've got. Therefore, you cannot permit sickness to stay in your body. From this position of having your heart fully persuaded, you take your authority as a child of God and curse that sickness to leave your body. It simply falls off your body. You have seen it in the word; you have seen it in your heart, now it has become a reality in your mouth. Now you are in FAITH! Remember, this is biblical faith and when you are in such unshakable assurance, no mountain can stand in your path[10].

The simple act of renewing your mind by participating in communion has the power to break the generational curses, genetic diseases, any other weakness or sickness in your body.

Your disease may have a genetic link. You may have inherited your disease from your earthly parents. But the truth is when you were born again; you were translated from the law of sin and death and placed under a superior divine law called the law of the spirit of life. Therefore, when you see yourself in Him, these diseases lose power over your life. Remember, those who are born again are born from above and they have access to supernatural laws of life.

The key is persuading your heart! Once your heart is fully persuaded to see His death as your death, then your mind will be illuminated with resurrection power. A mind that is convinced of the resurrection power will not accept sickness in the body. It will command the sickness to depart with absolute conviction.

What are you going to do now? How are you going to approach the communion table from now-on?

Scripture Reference

1. And when Jesus had cried out with a loud voice, He said, "Father, 'into Your hands I commit My spirit.' " Having said this, He breathed His last. Luke 23:46 NKJV
2. And so it is written, "The first man Adam became a living being." The last Adam *became* a life-giving spirit. 1 Corinthians 15:45 NKJV
3. But one of the soldiers pierced His side with a spear, and immediately blood and water came out. John 19:34 NKJV
4. For *it is* the life of all flesh. Its blood sustains its life. Therefore I said to the children of Israel, 'You shall not eat the blood of any flesh, for the life of all flesh is its blood. Whoever eats it shall be cut off.' Leviticus 17:14 NKJV
5. But you are not in the flesh but in the Spirit, if indeed the Spirit of God dwells in you. Now if anyone does not have the Spirit of Christ, he is not His. Romans 8:9 NKJV
6. And those *who are* Christ's have crucified the flesh with its passions and desires. Galatians 5:24 NKJV
7. For if we have been planted together in the likeness of his death, we shall be also in the likeness of his resurrection Romans 6:5 KJV
8. And raised *us* up together, and made *us* sit together in the heavenly *places* in Christ Jesus Ephesians 2:6 NKJV
9. He who eats My flesh and drinks My blood abides in Me, and I in him. John 6:56 NKJV
10. For assuredly, I say to you, whoever says to this mountain, 'Be removed and be cast into the sea,' and does not doubt in his heart, but believes that those things he says will be done, he will have whatever he says. Mark 11:23 NKJV

Chapter 9

WALKING IN THE SPIRIT

We have seen from the previous chapters that as soon as one is born again he or she is in the spirit. You are not in the flesh but in the Spirit, if indeed the Spirit of God dwells in you. Now if anyone does not have the Spirit of Christ, he is not His (Romans 8:9). However, to experience spirit-life in day to day living, we need to learn to walk in the spirit. The Galatian church believers who started off in the spirit soon started to get into legalism. Therefore, the Apostle Paul encouraged them to learn to walk in the spirit. The word *walk* here means 'to line up with.' What Paul was writing to them was that they should start to line up their beliefs and behaviours with their spirit[1]. This, in essence, is the core message of every New Testament writer. God has done His part and now we need to take responsibility and renew our mind and start to walk in line with our spirit. This is the battle of the mind which is also described in the Bible as *the good fight of faith.*

As I studied the scriptures for the healing of my body, I realised that I needed to take responsibility and learn to walk in the spirit otherwise I would squander what Grace had already provided. I also learnt that all things pertaining to life (health, healing and provision) are already given to me in Christ[2]. All I needed to do was learn how to appropriate this.

WALKING IN THE SPIRIT IS A WALK OF FAITH. From my study, I concluded that I will experience this only when I learn how to walk in the spirit. Failing to do so, I will not experience what God has already given me. It is either a walk of faith or stay put in defeat! There is no other option!

Walking in the spirit is a walk of faith. As simple as that! But what is faith? Faith is unshakable trust in the promises of God. Here is the catch: Faith only works within the boundaries of the beliefs of your heart. What you believe about yourself creates a boundary in your heart. Your faith will never go beyond that boundary. When "Christ in you" becomes the dominant thought of your life pertaining to a particular area, you have moved the boundary in your heart concerning that area. At the start of this journey, what you believed about yourself (perceived identity) and what God thinks about you (true identity) may have been different. As you stayed plugged in the word of God and renewed your mind, you would have noticed that the two identities began to merge into one. More and more you begin to see yourself as the way God sees you. This is transformation and also means you are travelling on the right path.

Our faith is anchored on what the Lord Jesus accomplished in His death, burial and resurrection. Therefore, faith is not wishful thinking nor it is fantasizing. Faith is unshakable trust in the finished work of Jesus. When you come to fully understand all that God made freely available for you through Jesus, then you are ready to move in faith. Faith comes from hearing the word[10]. The word *hearing* means

FAITH IS UNSHAKABLE TRUST IN THE FINISHED WORK OF JESUS.

unveiling; an unveiling of what Jesus has accomplished on the cross, and your true identity in Christ!

Faith starts with considering the promise of God. Because you are in Him, you are fully qualified to receive those promises[4]. Now, you can see the promises come alive in your heart. No more begging God, no more condemnation and no more disqualifying yourself by looking at your own works.

FAITH IN THE HEART

The word *faith* and the word *believe* are translated from the same Greek word which means *to see it in your heart as true NOW!* In the realm of faith there is no concept of time. That is the reason Jesus asked us to believe that we received when we pray and not when we see it with our eyes. To believe means to see with your heart!

An example will help us understand how to engage in the process. Let's say you have osteoarthritis (with severe knee pain). You know the promise of God which says; by His stripes, you are healed of all diseases. Jesus conquered your arthritis at His resurrection (remember, it was our sickness and diseases that were placed on him). When He rose from the dead, you also rose with Him. You in Him have conquered that arthritis.

Now, in your heart, you begin to see yourself pain-free, running, and jogging and doing all activities without any limitations. Remember, you are seeing this in your heart while doing meditation mentioned earlier. You are not faking this. Actually, you are seeing what is in your spirit and this is what God sees about you in the spirit. Joy and happiness fill your emotions as you keep seeing this image. You keep seeing yourself healed over and over again. You are trying to persuade your heart like how Abraham persuaded his heart. Then one day you see it clearly and start walking pain-free as this is the only reality that is established in your heart. This is the miracle power of your heart.

DOUBTING IN THE HEART

In the same example above, when you start seeing yourself in your heart severely limited by pain; you see yourself going to the doctor, and walking with the walking aid. You see yourself unable to run or walk or do any useful activity. Now you are in doubt. Only when you paint a negative picture contrary to the promise of God in your heart, you are in doubt. Fear begins to dominate your emotions. This image may be based on experiences of your own or other people's negative experiences. When you let anything other than God's word and His reality, dominate your imagination you are in doubt.

Just a fleeting negative thought doesn't mean you are in doubt. Seeing yourself crippled with pain in your heart is being in doubt. This is what Jesus meant, "To believe and not doubt in your heart" in the following scripture.

For assuredly, I say to you, whoever says to this mountain, 'Be removed and be cast into the sea,' and does not doubt in his heart, but believes that those things he says will be done, he will have whatever he says. Mark 11:23 NKJV

WAVERING

In the book of James, the Apostle James said that when we waver we will not receive anything from the Lord[5]. Wavering happens when you shift your focus back and forth between faith and doubt. I found myself wavering a lot as I started my healing journey. Remember, this is a road only a few are willing to take and therefore there aren't many in the church to encourage you along the way. The majority will blame the devil, blame God, and blame the circumstances and will stay put. All those are man-made circumstance theology to find an excuse for not labouring to persuade their heart with His word. Every biblical healing happened along these lines. I started to notice that when my heart was held in faith, I experienced healing in my body. Your heart will be persuaded when there is enough evidence. The cure for wavering is influencing your heart with strong evidence. Always remember, information plus emotion leads to writing of the truth in your heart. That is why in meditation, we need to see ourselves living those promises until it influences our emotion.

THE WORD IS THE EVIDENCE

Faith is the evidence of things hoped for! [11] The word *things* here refer to those things which are already accomplished for us by the death, burial and the resurrection of Jesus Christ. There is only one place to gather evidence and it's from the word of God. This is when I learnt to sanctify (set apart) myself from the distractions of the world and immerse myself in the word of God. I began to read and meditate on faith stories, like the story of David and Goliath and saw myself inside David defeating Goliath. Since we have the same spirit of faith[7], we can connect with faith stories in the Bible and encourage ourselves. This is the reason the Holy Spirit has recorded those stories in the Bible. If we are not connecting by faith with those stories, we are just reading a history book and we will not experience power.

Sanctifying yourself and immersing into the word is the only way to persuade your heart[8]. This may mean you stop indulging in television, social media and other time stealers. Listening to faith-filled messages from anointed preachers is good but you have to be careful to pick and choose whom you are listening. Be led by the Holy Spirit, if you don't feel peace in your heart, shut it down.

Your heart will believe for which it has more evidence. This is the way God has created your heart. This is the only way to positively influence your heart with God's word. Every biblical record of healing followed this pattern. When you study the Bible you will see that everyone who received healing had their hearts persuaded. Let us do a case study to verify that!

CASE STUDY - ABRAHAM - THE FATHER OF FAITH

Abraham was 100 years old and had lost the physiological capacity to bring forth a child. Moreover, Sarah also had attained menopause. There was no chance in their natural ability to bring forth a child. The outlook was pretty bleak. If we don't analyse this carefully, we will miss a very important lesson that will be useful for us. Abraham faced the fact that His body was dead[9]. However, he took God's spoken word of promise and painted another reality in his heart. His heart worked the miracle because he provided more evidence to his heart from the word.

Abraham knew God's word cannot be broken. He had walked with God for 25 years by that time. God had given him a word saying his children are going to be like the stars of the skies and the sand of the sea. In the imagination of his heart, he started seeing his children like the sand and like the stars. He was not fantasizing rather he was acting on God's word. It took a while for him to fully persuade His heart. That is the reason he agreed to have his name changed to Abraham, meaning father of many nations (before that he was called Abram

FAITH TAKES HOLD OF THE PROMISES OF GOD AND BRINGS IT INTO MANIFESTATION.

meaning exalted father). When his heart was fully persuaded, his faith brought forth the child. Faith took hold of the promises of God and brought it into manifestation. It's the miracle of the heart. It's that simple!

James said he who wavers let him not suppose that he will receive anything from the Lord. The word *receive* in the Greek is not a passive waiting for God to show up someday in the future. That word *receive* means to take hold of that which is promised and bring it into manifestation. This is exactly what Abraham did. This is the walk of faith!

You are already healed in Christ when He rose from the dead! And your life is hidden in Him. Now grab hold of it and bring it into manifestation. The devil will throw everything at you to stop you from persuading your heart. He knows what you will become once your heart is fully persuaded. You will destroy his kingdom. The devil is scared of you! Even if someone is operating in the "gift of healing", you will only receive from them along the lines I have mentioned above. This is the reason even Jesus could not heal everyone, as they were in unbelief. When you are in doubt about the promises of God, you are in unbelief. The good news is that you can change your heart.

THE MOST POWERFUL WEAPON OF THE HEART IS THE SHIELD OF FAITH.

Every disciple of the Lord Jesus is destined to live this way. The Holy Spirit will constantly guide you. Nothing pleases the heart of the Father more than to see His loving children embrace His ways and to walk by faith. This is the way every renowned men and women of the Bible had walked.

FIGHTING THE GOOD FIGHT

Many are fighting the wrong fight on the wrong turf. The devil is the father of lies. He feeds us with lies. All lies are darkness!. On the other hand, the word truth is equated to light. We resist the devil by not shouting at him; rather we speak the truth in our hearts. Speaking the truth in our heart means, to frame a picture in our heart based on God's promises. Truth, which is light, dispels darkness. When our mind (conscious and subconscious) is fully illuminated with truth, the body will be full of light. We are called to fight the good fight of faith and this fight is a battle waged in our mind. In writing to Timothy, Paul encouraged him to fight the good fight of faith and to

HELL IS AFTER YOUR TONGUE

lay hold of eternal life[10]. To lay hold means to take a firm grip of what is already inside you. Once you change the image of how you see yourself inside you, the war is over. You enter into His rest. This is the only warfare we are supposed to wage in the new covenant. Remember, the devil was annihilated by our Lord at the cross. Now we participate in His victory through faith[11].

In your pursuit to persuade your heart, one of the most important things you should be aware of is taking every thought into captivity to the obedience of Christ[12]. One thing that will fight you till the very end is self-righteousness. Instead of keeping your eyes on Jesus all the time, the devil will try his best to distract you and to shift your eyes on to your good performances. Remember, it's all about His obedience and not ours. Every thought needs to be filtered through the cross. At the end of the day, it's all about Him and seeing yourself complete in Him. Paul said we do not fight with carnal weapons rather powerful weapons. The most powerful weapon of the heart is the shield of faith. Faith is compared to a shield in the list of the armour of God described in the book of Ephesians[13]. It's a very apt description of faith. You see, when the positive picture is fully set in your heart, anything contrary to that picture the devil may throw at you simply won't penetrate. The heart will be hardened with the word of God which will function as a shield. Like Jesus Himself, your every step will be governed by the word of God. This is the walk of the spirit!

CONFESSION OF YOUR MOUTH

Having understood clearly how faith works, now let us turn our attention to another important area - Confession of your mouth!

People, who jumped into "confession" without establishing their hearts in faith, experienced a backlash. Sadly, because of that, the confession of God's word which should have been healthy has gotten a bad name. Confession should be an overflow of your heart. Faith-filled words are just an overflow of a heart that is established in the Word. Words are powerful and sadly in our society words have lost their value, nevertheless, we are experiencing their effects even without fully realizing it. According to Jesus, words are a spirit! (John 6:63)

Like the laws of physics that govern the natural world, there are laws of the spirit that govern the spirit led life. The Law of the Spirit operates mostly through the confession of faith-filled words. Jesus said:

For assuredly, I say to you, whoever **says** to this mountain, 'Be removed and be cast into the sea,' and does not doubt in his heart, but believes that those things he **says** will be done, he will have whatever he **says**. Mark 11:23 NKJV emphasis mine

In the above scripture, Jesus gives us wisdom which is oftentimes neglected. The power is released when we say it! However, unless one believes and sees himself as a mountain mover in his heart, no amount of speaking to the mountain will work. The mouth and the heart should function as one unit. It is from this place, you can speak to your situation and it will obey you. The key is saying, but not merely voicing words, but saying from the heart that is already set on His word.

A wholesome tongue *is* a tree of life, but perverseness in it breaches the spirit (Proverbs 15:4). Remember, the tree of life is already in your spirit. When you were born again, the Word of God, which is the tree of life, was planted in your heart. A wholesome tongue is a tongue that aligns its words with what is already in the spirit. A

YOUR TONGUE IS INCREDIBLY POWERFUL

wholesome tongue speaks God's word in every situation. On the other hand, a perverse tongue is a tongue which speaks what's in the carnal mind and will not line up with the spirit. By doing that, it cuts off the spirit-life. This is what it means *a perverse tongue breaches the spirit.*

Your words are powerful. Sadly, I did not understand the power of my tongue for years. Now that I do, I am very cautious because I can release blessings or curses with my tongue. It's a weapon and I need to be careful about how I use it. Death and life are in the power of your tongue. The Apostle James gave us a sound warning about the danger of the tongue. James said hell is after our tongue (James 3:6), meaning the devil wants us to speak his words; words of fear and doubt. Remember, the devil is the flesh devil. The carnal mind is the seat of the flesh. Therefore, the devil wants you to speak words from your carnal mind and not from your heart where the Spirit of God lives. Now you know why you have to be careful with your tongue. With your tongue, you should bless your body and release life every day.

YOUR HEART AND YOUR TONGUE SHOULD FUNCTION AS ONE UNIT

If you are a person given to gossiping and chatting, you should learn to quieten down. Because wisdom says, in the multitudes of words sin is not lacking[14]. Chatting will eventually lead you into the realm of the flesh and the one who talks a lot ends up speaking foolishness. Death is packed in our jokes and comments that tickles our senses. When one realizes that they are spiritual beings living in a body, then he or she can truly appreciate the power of words. A soul that is surrendered to the spirit is very careful to throw words. Your tongue is incredibly powerful and it can release life or death. Therefore, use it wisely and speak His word from your heart.

Walking in the spirit is not something that we master overnight. It's the way of the disciple and it's the joyful journey of a lifetime. It's a walk whereby you take one situation at a time and learn to yield to the Holy Spirit as He gently leads you beside the still waters and green pastures.

Walking in faith (spirit) involves these 4 simple steps,

1. First, see the promises of God in the Word, and see yourself qualified for that promise (as you are in Christ).
2. Based on that promise, now you paint a picture of your life healthy and whole in your heart through meditation.
3. You align your tongue to that which you have already seen in your heart.
4. Now you act according to what you have seen and spoken.

This is the only way to persuade your heart! There is no other way!

GUARDING THE GARDEN

Thorns and snares are in the way of the perverse;
He who guards his soul will be far from them.

Proverbs 22:5 NKJV

The word *perverse* also means crooked or distorted. From our study of the heart, we know the soul is a part of our heart which we can influence. So the wisdom of God is saying if you want to avoid thorns and snares in your life, we should guard your heart against distortion. The spirit part is already made right with God. If we don't keep our mind and our tongue in line with our spirit, then we create distortions. This is the reason for all the misery in a believer's life!

THE ONLY WAY TO DEAL WITH FLESH IS: DEATH!

When you walk in the spirit you judge yourself in the light of God's word. You see yourself qualified as you are in Him. It's from this perspective you can see other fellow believers in the spirit as well. You see them as qualified as you are. This will help a great deal in avoiding offence and also to walk in love. Faith works through love. A walk of the spirit is a walk of love.

When Jesus said; "first you should remove the speck from your own eye[15]," He is talking about learning to see your-self in the spirit first, and then, only then you can see and judge others correctly. Paul echoes the same thought when writing to the Corinthian believers who were walking carnally[16]. Paul encouraged them to see themselves in the spirit! Jesus was not talking about cleaning our flesh, when it comes to dealing with the flesh there is no cleansing possible. There is only one way to deal with the flesh: Death! The only way to not to fulfil the lust of the flesh is to walk after the spirit. There is no in between and there is no other way!

PUT OFF - PUT ON

Paul encourages believers in all his epistles to put off those things that were programmed by the old man and put on the new man who is created in true righteousness and holiness[17]. This is a very simple yet powerful practical advice we can practice every day. As you are in Christ, you can exercise your authority over those tormenting thoughts, unforgiveness and all those negative emotions that bother you. During your quiet time of meditation, you speak firmly to those thoughts and send them away. See those thoughts leave in your imagination. As soon as you have spoken, you know they have to leave because you are speaking from the position of having known who you are in Christ. Any time they come back to you, you simply remind yourself that you have cast them out. Many times it is that simple!

Once you have sent those thoughts away, you replace your mind with thoughts that are healthy and positive concerning your identity from the Word. Mark all those scriptures which says; in Christ, through Christ, and with Christ in your Bible and confess them regularly. You always speak in the first person singular. The Psalmist David did this exercise often. He kept telling himself how good God is and how awesome His acts were in the past. You see he was putting on the Lord Jesus, so to speak. Jesus gave us the keys of the kingdom of God. Kingdom also means realm! The realm of the spirit works from your heart through your mouth.

I will give you the keys (authority) of the kingdom of heaven; and whatever you bind [forbid, declare to be improper and unlawful] on earth will have [already] been bound in heaven, and whatever you lose [permit, declare lawful] on earth will have [already] been loosed in heaven." Matthew 16:18 AMP

The Amplified Bible spells it out clearly as to how the keys of the kingdom work. It works by us permitting or not permitting things that concern our lives. We use words to declare and order our steps, words that line up with our spirit. This is the crux of walking in the spirit!

Fear and dread is very tormenting. When you step out in faith you will have to face your fears. The biggest fear is the fear of death. Fear of death is nothing more than the fear of the unknown. Thoughts of fear are the fiery darts the enemy will shoot at you as you step out in faith. You have the authority and you have to exercise it. Every fearful thought you should send it away to the cross. I have taught my children to exercise put-off put-on and send the offences away to the cross. Once my daughter commented; "so daddy, the cross is like a magnet that pulls bad things to itself as we send it away." I could not have put it any clearer than that. Yes, erect a cross in the midst of the garden of your heart in your imagination and as you send them away, see the cross attracting all those negative thoughts, feelings and emotions to it-self.

DEALING WITH UN-FORGIVENESS

Jesus instructs us to walk in forgiveness over our offenders. Sometimes, It's been erroneously preached that if one doesn't forgive their offenders, then God will not forgive them either. Such teachings are floating around because of a lack of understanding of the finished work of Jesus, and also because of the misunderstanding of what Jesus said in certain places in the Bible. In the Lord's Prayer, Jesus said, "Forgive us our sins as we forgive those who trespass against us". From this statement, people have concluded that God will not forgive us if we don't forgive others. In another place also Jesus said it this way,

> "And whenever you stand praying, if you have anything against anyone, forgive him that your Father in heaven may also forgive you your trespasses. 26 But if you do not forgive, neither will your Father in heaven forgive your trespasses." Mark 11:25–26 NKJV

There it is in black and white! It appears in the 26th verse Jesus says; that the father in heaven will not forgive us if we don't forgive others from our heart. But wait! Hold on! Let's for a moment think about what we have studied so far about the cross! You see God forgave the sins of the whole world when Christ was raised from the dead. All the sins of all the people of the whole world are forgiven at the cross! Does it mean all are saved? NO!

Releasing forgiveness is a one person act, whereas reconciliation is a two–person act. God released forgiveness for the whole world at the CROSS so that men can call upon the Lord Jesus and receive the forgiveness and be reconciled with God. This is the astounding announcement of the gospel of Jesus Christ. Look at the following scripture written by the Apostle Paul,

> Now all things *are* of God, who has reconciled us to Himself through Jesus Christ, and has given us the

ministry of reconciliation, that is, **that God was in Christ reconciling the world to Himself, not imputing their trespasses to them**, and has committed to us the word of reconciliation. Now then, we are ambassadors for Christ, as though God were pleading through us: we implore *you* on Christ's behalf, be reconciled to God. 2 Corinthians 5:18-20 NKJV emphasis mine

Our sins are imputed on Jesus and therefore God is not imputing our trespasses on us! All our sins are forgiven on the cross! Now, God is inviting the whole world to receive His forgiveness and be reconciled with Him. So, how do we square this understanding with what Jesus said in Mark 11:26? Remember, the power of God resides in our spirit. If we don't forgive others, it's like we erect a wall between our spirit and soul. Therefore, the life and healing that is in our spirit no longer can flow from within out. So, Jesus is giving us wisdom to let go of offences so that we can experience the flow of God from our spirit. If someone has offended you, and that you are struggling to forgive that person then talk to your heavenly Father about it. Confess it before Him and let Him strengthen you. Once you are convinced that His forgiveness is unconditional and it resides inside you, it's easy to release forgiveness to other. At that point you can release the offender by saying, "Lord, in your name I release this person from my heart and his/her offence to the cross". I send away the hurt feelings and put-on the love of Christ which is inside me, in my spirit. I choose to walk in freedom. Amen! This is how you do it by faith. Remember, your feelings may not be in agreement, however, this is the walk of faith. Your feelings will follow later. If needed take communion and see those offences go away from you to the cross. Put-on, put-off is a biblical way of walking the resurrection life to experience healing in every area.

Scripture Reference

1. If we live in the Spirit, let us also walk in the Spirit. Galatians 5:25 NKJV
2. As His divine power has given to us all things that pertain to life and godliness, through the knowledge of Him who called us by glory and virtue. 2 Peter 1:3 NKJV
3. So then faith comes by hearing, and hearing by the word of God. Romans 10:17 NKJV
4. For all the promises of God in Him are Yes, and in Him Amen, to the glory of God through us. 2 Corinthians 1:20 NKJV
5. For let not that man suppose that he will receive anything from the Lord; he is a double-minded man, unstable in all his ways. James 1:7-8 NKJV
6. Now faith is the substance of things hoped for, the evidence of things not seen. 2 For by it the elders obtained a good testimony. Hebrews 11:1 NKJV
7. And since we have the same spirit of faith, according to what is written, "I believed and therefore I spoke," we also believe and therefore speak. 2 Corinthians 4:13 NKJV
8. Therefore, laying aside all malice, all deceit, hypocrisy, envy, and all evil speaking, as new-born babes, desire the pure milk of the word, that you may grow thereby. 1 Peter 2:1-2 NKJV
9. Without weakening in his faith, he faced the fact that his body was as good as dead—since he was about a hundred years old—and that Sarah's womb was also dead. Yet he did not waver through unbelief regarding the promise of God, but was strengthened in his faith and gave glory to God. Romans 4:19-20 NIV
10. Fight the good fight of faith, lay hold on eternal life, to which you were also called and have confessed the good confession in the presence of many witnesses. 1 Timothy 6:12 NKJV
11. For whatever is born of God overcomes the world. And this is the victory that has overcome the world—our faith. 1 John 5:4 NKJV
12. For the weapons of our warfare are not carnal but mighty in God for pulling down strongholds, casting down arguments and every high thing that exalts itself against the knowledge of

God, bringing every thought into captivity to the obedience of Christ. 2 Corinthians 10:4-5 NKJV

13. Above all, taking the shield of faith with which you will be able to quench all the fiery darts of the wicked one. Ephesians 6:16 NKJV

14. In the multitude of words sin is not lacking, But he who restrains his lips is wise. Proverbs 10:18 NKJV

15. And why do you look at the speck in your brother's eye, but do not consider the plank in your own eye? Or how can you say to your brother, 'Let me remove the speck from your eye'; and look, a plank is in your own eye? Hypocrite! First remove the plank from your own eye, and then you will see clearly to remove the speck from your brother's eye. Matthew 7:3-5 NKJV

16. But the natural man does not receive the things of the Spirit of God, for they are foolishness to him; nor can he know them, because they are spiritually discerned. But he who is spiritual judges all things, yet he himself is rightly judged by no one. 1 Corinthians 2:14-15 NKJV

17. That you put off, concerning your former conduct, the old man which grows corrupt according to the deceitful lusts, and be renewed in the spirit of your mind, and that you put on the new man which was created according to God, in true righteousness and holiness. Ephesians 4:22-24 NKJV

Chapter 10

ENTERING INTO HIS REST

We see in the creation story in Genesis that God rested on the seventh day. Man was created on the sixth day and entered into God's rest. The Sabbath was a picture of this rest. In the Ten Commandments, the fourth commandment is to remember the Sabbath day[1]. This was given as a reminder to look forward to the Messiah who will give true rest. Everything that is needed for Adam was provided in the Garden of Eden. Adam enjoyed a life of fellowship with God in an environment of peace and tranquillity. This is the perfect will of God for mankind. We who are born again are expecting new heaven and new earth at a future date when the Lord returns and our hearts are filled with hope and joy. But before that day comes, our Lord has not left us helpless now.

He has established a kingdom within us. We are called to enter into that kingdom and experience rest now.

Ever since man fell from his glorious state, God has been trying to get us to enter into that rest. The idea of rest is an alien concept for a religious legalistic and externalist mind. In the book of Hebrews, in chapter four the writer points out that there remains a rest for the people of God. In the Old Testament, the Promise Land was a type of rest for the children of Israel, yet that was not the true rest. Joshua led the Israelites into the Promised Land. If that was the true rest, then David, who came years after Joshua, would not have spoken of another day of rest in the future. You see, the true rest was always Jesus. Jesus is the central point of all creation both in heaven and on the earth. All things were created for Him, in Him and through Him[2]. The Promise Land was a type and shadow of the true rest which was to come and now that rest is available in Jesus.

WE LABOUR TO ENTER INTO THE REST.

In the same chapter, we see that the writer of Hebrews is calling the believers to labour to enter the rest. This is one of the paradoxes of living by faith. We labour to enter into rest! Once we enter the rest, the labouring stops. When you read that chapter carefully, it looks like the writer has changed the topic between the 11th and the 12th verse.

[11] Let us therefore be diligent to enter that rest, lest anyone fall according to the same example of disobedience.

[12] For the word of God *is* living and powerful, and sharper than any two-edged sword, piercing even to the division of soul and spirit, and of joints and marrow, and is a discerner of the thoughts and intents of the heart. Hebrews 4:11–12 NKJV

In the 11th verse, he is calling all believers to be diligent to enter that rest, and in the 12th verse he is talking about the life of God's Word. It's not a change in topic. You see the true rest the Bible promises for every child of God in the new covenant is the word of God. The Promised land for a new covenant believer is the promises of God! When we live by the promises of God we truly enter into His rest. From studying the previous chapters, you have understood that faith righteousness is a gift. So we are not labouring to become righteous, rather, we are labouring to yield to the power of righteousness. When we do that, righteousness begins to permeate into our thoughts, feelings, behaviour and our health.

IT IS IMPOSSIBLE TO WALK IN SICKNESS WHEN YOUR HEART IS FULLY PERSUADED IN THE PROMISES OF GOD

It's impossible to walk in sickness and disease when your heart is fully persuaded in the promises of God. This is the labouring we are called to do. This is done through the renewing of our mind. Therefore, the renewing of your mind is the beginning of the transformation and experiencing true rest.

Let us examine another scripture.

His divine power has given us everything we need for a godly life through our knowledge of Him who called us by his own glory and goodness. Through these he has given us his **very great and precious promises**, so that through them you may participate in the **divine nature**, having escaped the corruption in the world caused by evil desires. 1 Peter 1:3-4 NIV emphasis mine

We have been given very great and precious promises! We are in Christ and therefore we are qualified for those promises. We are worthy in Him to participate in the goodness of God. Now we

YOU DON'T HAVE A SIN NATURE. YOU HAVE A DIVINE NATURE IN CHRIST.

start to labour; we see ourselves living those promises in our hearts. As we stay focused on those promises, those promises pertaining to a particular situation become the reality in our heart. At that point, we have entered into His rest. We have persuaded our heart. Only then it begins to manifest in our lives.

SIN NATURE OR DIVINE NATURE

Many believers are confused about these terms and some believe that they have a sin nature even after they are born again. According to the word of God you don't have a sin nature; rather, you have a divine nature. You have to settle this matter in your heart. If this is not the starting point, then you will never start the journey at all. You are translated from darkness into light[3]. Your sin nature is gone. In its place, you have a divine nature. God is calling us to participate in the divine nature through His promises. Remember, however, you have a flesh. As we saw in the previous chapters, the flesh is crucified with Christ. Therefore we are not trying to crucify our flesh. We simply accept the death of our flesh in the death of Jesus. When we take communion, we proclaim our death in His death so that we arrive at the resurrection life. Entering into His rest is an invitation for every one of us. Only in rest we will experience and enjoy health as it should be (righteousness). Therefore, let us be diligent to enter into His rest!

BEING FILLED IN THE SPIRIT

To experience the promise of God as real in our hearts, we need to understand how to be filled in the spirit. Many have misunderstood being filled in the spirit to be some sort of a mystic and have deviated from the Apostles' doctrine. Some church groups are totally avoiding the spirit because of the picture that's being portrayed in the name of being filled in the spirit. Being filled in the spirit has become elusive to many and some equate speaking in tongues as being filled in the spirit. This is not entirely correct. Rather, praying in unknown tongues is the overflow of being filled in the spirit. On the day of Pentecost, they were all filled in the Spirit first and then they began to speak in another tongue.

The Apostle Paul gave us insight as to how to be filled in the spirit in his writings to the Ephesian church. Writing about it, he said, "Do not be drunk with wine but you be filled in the spirit by speaking to yourself in psalms, hymns,

185

and spiritual songs, making melody unto the Lord and be thankful[4]." This is the biblical way to be filled in the spirit. When we constantly remind ourselves of who we are and connect to that reality through singing and worshipping and making melody in our hearts unto Jesus (who lives inside us), we put on the spirit-reality in our mind. Then the life of God begins to flood our emotions and thoughts and we are filled in the spirit. Then as we yield our tongue to this overwhelming flow of the spirit, we begin to speak words from the spirit. This is what Jesus precisely meant in the following verse.

> But whoever drinks of the water that I shall give him will never thirst. But the water that I shall give him will become in him a fountain of water springing up into everlasting life. John 4:14 NKJV

Note: It's springing up, meaning, it is bubbling from the inside.

David wrote Psalms from being filled in the spirit. After he was anointed by the prophet Samuel, the Bible says that the spirit of God came upon him mightily from that day onwards[5]. He had great insight into the life of the Messiah, and in no other way he could have received those insights except by the Holy Spirit. When we read psalms and begin to speak to ourselves we connect with the Holy Spirit who lives inside us. This is a transformation process which one can readily experience once they establish their hearts in faith righteousness. There is power in meditating on the book of Psalms!

THE POWER OF PRAYING IN TONGUES

When God called me into full time ministry, He led me into a season of praying in tongues. So, I found myself praying for hours in tongues. Though I did not understand what I was praying, but this I knew that when I prayed in tongues I was praying mysteries (1 Corinthians 14:1-3). My mind was screaming with boredom so I would play some music on the background, and sometimes I would read bible and other times I would simply copy scriptures on my diary, all this while I was still praying in tongues. Praying in tongues is a very important aspect of walking in the spirit. The gift of tongues is

FASTING BREAKS THE POWER OF THE CARNAL MIND

oftentimes under-used in the body of Christ. Scientific research has shown that when one speaks in tongues, they bypass the part of the brain which is involved in active thinking. In other words, tongues get us into a state of deep relaxation. When the mind relaxes the whole body relaxes. This is what God promised in the book of Isaiah.

Very well then, with foreign lips and strange tongues God will speak to this people, to whom he said, "This is the resting place, let the weary rest"; and, "This is the place of repose"— Isaiah 28:11-12 NKJV

Praying in tongues is a God-given way of rest because we pray and sing from the spirit. Especially coupled with a mind focused on the promises of God we experience transformation. This is one of the new covenant ways of praying! Therefore, let us labour to enter into His rest through the gift of *tongues.*

FASTING

Fasting is an incredible tool to aid in the renewal of the mind. Remember, in labouring, you are trying to persuade your heart and establishing it in the promises of God. You are focused and dedicated so that the promises of God become more real than the pain or any other symptoms of your disease. When asked about fasting, Jesus replied this...

But the days will come when the bridegroom will be taken away from them, and then they will fast in those days. No one sews a piece of unshrunk cloth on an old garment; or else the new piece pulls away from the old, and the tear is made worse. And no one puts new wine into old wineskins; or else the new wine bursts the wineskins, the wine is spilled, and the wineskins are ruined. But new wine must be put into new wineskins."
Mark 2: 20–22 NKJV

The new piece of cloth and the new wine represent the dynamic nature of a spirit-filled life. This is the spirit we have received in the new birth. However, the old mind-set is rigid like old cloth and the old wineskin. An old mindset will not flow with the dynamism of the new spirit. Jesus is giving incredible wisdom as to how to change the old mindset. Fasting!

Your mind has developed all these years from the information gained through the five senses: sight, smell, hearing, taste and touch. When you fast, you should aim to fast from/of all these senses. Sanctifying your-self from watching television, social media or reading anything other than the word of God, coupled with fasting of food is a powerful way to break the power of the carnal mind. Also, you are now equipping your mind with new information from the word of God. This breaks the mind which has been working in the world system. Doing this regularly brings the mind alive to the spirit inside you. You begin to flow in the spirit more fluently. This is the way of a disciple.

The benefits of entering and staying in God's rest are a life of peace and joy. This is the paradox of living the resurrected life, we labour and yet we rest. It sounds like we are giving up so much, but the truth is we are gaining the ways of God. This is true freedom. The ways of God is life and peace for His children. This is the way you were destined to live all these years and now you are finding it out. Your heart is already leaping with joy unspeakable and full of Glory.

And so we have the prophetic word confirmed, which you do well to heed as a light that shines in a dark place, until the day dawns and the morning star rises in your hearts. 1 Peter 1:19 NKJV

As you engage in the process of renewing your mind, you will experience the light getting brighter in increasing proportions like the dawning of the day, and at some point, the morning star (Jesus) will rise in your heart. Meaning, Christ in you becomes the dominant reality in your heart. You will see the life of Jesus so clearly in your heart that there is no separation of Him from you. His victory becomes yours. His health becomes yours. Now you have arrived into

His rest. This is the place where you lose yourself completely in Him. The demarcation line between where you stop and He begins will be erased!

Scripture Reference

1. Remember the Sabbath day, to keep it holy. Exodus 20:8 NKJV

2. He is the image of the invisible God, the firstborn over all creation. For by Him all things were created that are in heaven and that are on earth, visible and invisible, whether thrones or dominions or principalities or powers. All things were created through Him and for Him. And He is before all things, and in Him all things consist. Colossians 1:17–18 NKJV

3. He has delivered us from the power of darkness and conveyed us into the kingdom of the Son of His love, in whom we have redemption through His blood, the forgiveness of sins. Colossians 1:13-14 NKJV

4. And do not be drunk with wine, in which is dissipation; but be filled with the Spirit, speaking to one another in psalms and hymns and spiritual songs, singing and making melody in your heart to the Lord, giving thanks always for all things to God the Father in the name of our Lord Jesus Christ. Ephesians 5:18-20 NKJV

5. Then Samuel took the horn of oil and anointed David in the presence of his brothers; and the Spirit of the Lord came mightily upon David from that day forward. And Samuel arose and went to Ramah. 1 Samuel 16:13 AMP

Conclusion

You have just begun the life of transformation! When you started this book, your sole intention was to get healed in your body and mind, but now the goal has changed. Now you desire to walk in divine health. Your heart is leaping with joy, the joy of having found your true identity in Christ. *Release your healing* is just not a title, rather, it's going to be the way of life for you and through you, to others.

The Holy Spirit is the one who transforms us but He cannot do it without our cooperation. Transformation is what happens when one beholds the Lord. To behold means to look with intent and purpose and just not a casual glance. It's important that we come to fully understand that He lives in us. In 2 Corinthians 3:18, the Apostle Paul said we behold Him as in a mirror. The mirror of God's word reflects the Christ who lives inside us. This is the starting point of true change! We start our journey beholding Him and we arrive when we understand that we are complete in Him. Anything we try to do, to become complete, is an empty philosophy and doctrine of the world system said the Apostle Paul (Colossians 2: 8).

You are armed with this incredible knowledge of what actually happened at the cross and because of that what has really happened to you. You no longer look at the word of God the same way as before. Now you know, the word is your true identity. What the word says about you is the true reality. Now you know how to take those realities found in the word and make it your heart belief by meditation. You have found the key to transformation. You desire to spend more time reading His word and renewing your mind. Your fight with the devil, circumstances and other time wasters are over. Now, you understand what the Apostle John said: "You have already overcome them because He that is in you is greater than he that is in the world." *Them* in this scripture refers to all the evil spirits. Now you don't want to waste your time fighting the devil, all you need to do is renew your mind. You also understood that strongholds are not demons, but the thoughts that are holding you in captivity; thoughts which are contrary to your true identity.

In this incredible journey, you realize following Jesus as the Lord of your life is no longer a threat, but a joy. You are more than happy to let go of your opinion and take His opinion found in His word. This is true surrender! You have become a true disciple and repentance has become a way of life for you.

Listening to the voice of the Holy Spirit has tremendous advantages in life. You are walking no longer as the rest of the gentiles walk. You are no longer alienated from the life of God which is inside you. You have arrived at the place of rest. In Him you are Complete! Now you look to

Christ for everything, He has become your life and there is no separation of you from Him.

You have discovered the keys of the kingdom. Unlike the residents of the pool of Bethesda (we read in John chapter 5) who were waiting for the next disturbance of the water by an angel to get healed, you are not waiting for the next move of God to happen. You have discovered that *the revival* is inside you. You have realised that you are the light of the world and you are ready to let it shine. Seeking the kingdom has become a top priority and all those worries about your life have evaporated. This is the abundant life Jesus promised.

As you are persuading your heart to establish yourself in the true identity, you may stumble, but you won't stay that way. You have learnt to commune with God in the spirit and He will guide you continually. Remember, Jesus is your shepherd, and as a good shepherd, He is proactively leading you every step of the way. If you miss Him, you are quick to realize that and reconnect with Him.

You have learnt the importance of having accurate knowledge. You also learnt the importance of guarding your heart. Any sermon and song that is not in line with the truth you will reject it now. This is a healthy way to live. You are not judgmental, but you are sensitive about guarding your heart. This is the wisdom of the master (Mark 4:24).

Influencing your heart with God's word has become your top priority. You don't want to spend any more time on mindless religious activities. All the scripture that you have memorised since childhood days have become very useful to you now. In fact, they are exploding in your heart as you read this. This is the work of the Holy Spirit. You have been destined to travel this road of faith since the foundation of the world, and now you have discovered it. There is no stopping you now!

There are four pillars of life which everyone is constantly building their lives upon. These are Health, Wealth, Career and Relationship. The currency that one uses to build these four domains is TIME. If you spend your time in His presence, all the four domains will take care of themselves. Remember what Jesus said, "All these things will be added to those who seek His kingdom first." Seeking His kingdom first means to live a life with a top priority to walk in the spirit! Now you have found the value of spending time with your heavenly Father. Your life is projected to a different plane. This is the joy of living from your heart.

Living from the heart is the secret of a successful Christian life. Many take the broad way, but now you have found the narrow way which is inside your heart. Take communion as often as you can because it's an incredible way to wrap your thoughts around the death, burial and resurrection of the Lord Jesus. Our goal is to experience the resurrection life, one situation at a time!

Last Few Words

In one of his best-selling books, "The knowledge of the Holy", AW Tozer writes this, "God is holy and He has made holiness the moral condition necessary to the health of His universe. Sin's temporary presence in the world only accents this. **Whatever is holy is healthy**; evil is a moral sickness that must end ultimately in death. The formation of the language itself suggests this, the English word *holy* deriving from the Anglo-Saxon *halig, hal*, meaning. "Well, whole." (Emphasis mine)

"Holy" means wholesome or complete! When God said *be Holy for I am holy*, He is not threatening us; rather, he is inviting us to participate in His wholeness through Christ! The Apostle Paul put it this way, "And in Him you are Complete." We learn to see ourselves complete in Him in every area of our lives by renewing our mind, one challenge at a time!

Now, remember this: You are COMPLETE in Him!

7 Key Scriptures

In this section, I have put together few key scriptures with my commentary under them in brackets. These scriptures helped me in my time of need. I believe this will help you too!

"He himself bore our sins" in his body on the cross, so that we might die to sins and live for righteousness; "by his wounds you have been healed." 1 Peter 2:24 NIV

(Here, Peter makes it very clear that we have already been healed. This happened at the cross. Now, all that is needed is for us to renew our mind and make that a reality in our heart.)

Beloved, I pray that in every way you may succeed *and* prosper and be in good health [physically], just as [I know] your soul prospers [spiritually]. 3 John 1:2 AMP

(John makes it very clear that as we renew our mind and change our image inside, then it will manifest in health and other areas too)

If Christ lives in you, though your [natural] body is dead because of sin, your spirit is alive because of righteousness [which He provides]. And if the Spirit of Him who raised Jesus from the dead lives in you, He who raised Christ Jesus from the dead will also give life to your mortal bodies through His Spirit, who lives in you. Romans 8:10–11 AMP

(This was a revolutionary scripture for me. This changed my entire attitude towards heath. The Holy Spirit is the key person in a Christian's life. He will educate you and make your mind sharp so that your lifestyle itself becomes healthy. Our every cell is sustained by the life of the Spirit.)

For if you eat the bread or drink the cup without honoring the body of Christ, you are eating and drinking God's judgment upon yourself. That is why many of you are weak and sick and some have even died. 1 Corinthians 11:29–30 NLT

(As I have already explained in the chapter on The Lord's Table, you have to see your sickness go in the Lord's body. This is the only way to honour His body today.)

My child, pay attention to what I say. Listen carefully to my words. Don't lose sight of them. Let them penetrate deep into your heart, for they bring life to those who find them, and healing to their whole body. Proverbs 4:20–23 NLT

(Trying to live independent of God's word is like disconnecting life from its source. If you take fish out of the water, it will die. Likewise if you don't plug yourself in His word, you will wither.)

**A wholesome tongue *is* a tree of life,
But perverseness in it breaks the spirit.
Proverbs 15:4 NKJV**

(Tongue is powerful and it carries the power to stop or release the life of the spirit. We have to constantly remind ourselves of this. Once the heart is renewed, your words will automatically line up with the heart.)

**Death and life *are* in the power of the tongue,
And those who love it will eat its fruit. Proverbs 18:20 NKJV**

(Tongue is a powerful weapon. Keep speaking life and blessing over your situation relentlessly. Your tongue was given to chart the course of your life. So, use it wisely!)

About The Author

Andrew grew up in India and became a Christian at the age of 17. He did his medical degree and post-graduation in Anaesthesia in India and further completed his FRCA from the Royal College of Anaesthetist, London. He enjoyed working as a consultant in Anaesthesia & Intensive care medicine in National Health Services, England. It was at the pinnacle of his career God called him to ministry; to teach and preach the gospel of Jesus Christ. Andrew heeded to the call immediately and resigned from his job to become a minister of the New Covenant. Today, Andrew functions as an Associate Pastor in his local church and also travels the world sharing the love of Jesus Christ to small groups, camp meetings, and churches.

He conducts *healing school* and *seminars on healing* in partnership with local churches around the world.

He is married to his lovely wife Nisha and lives with their two children Samuel and Ruth in England, United Kingdom.

For healing school and weekend healing workshops contact Andrew directly.

Contact: releaseyourhealing@gmail.com

Books by Andrew

1. The Secret Place
2. Release Your Healing
3. Divine Healing–A Study Guide

Printed in Poland
by Amazon Fulfillment
Poland Sp. z o.o., Wrocław

52656821R00122